A READER'S COMPANION
TO GEORGE FOX'S JOURNAL

Seventeenth-Century hour-glass in a Church in Berkshire

This hour-glass normally stands in a wrought iron holder fixed to the edge of the pulpit, in view of the congregation. Hour-glasses were commonly used in churches in the sixteenth and seventeenth centuries for recording time. They reserved a period of time to the preacher. Interrupters were punished—see p. 41, St.1 Mary c.6; p. 44, 1655. See p. 24/5–26, 76/10–32; also Concordance, **time(3).**

A
Reader's Companion
to
George Fox's Journal

By
Joseph Pickvance

QUAKER HOME SERVICE

First published June 1989
by Quaker Home Service
Friends House, Euston Road, London NW1 2BJ

The cover illustration of Swarthmoor Hall is a detail
from a watercolour by Constance D Pearson
and is reproduced here by permission
of Friends House Library

Printed in Great Britain in Times 10/12
by Headley Brothers Ltd, Invicta Press,
Ashford, Kent and London

Contents

Appendices

Preface

When I began to compile material for this Reader's Companion, the Nickalls *Journal* was the only Fox text in print. So, although I was aware of its limitations as a source of George Fox's teaching, I had no choice but to make the best use of it I could. In the past ten years two selections from Fox's *Epistles* (1698) have appeared—Cecil Sharman's *No More But My Love* (1980) and the Friends United Press reprint of Samuel Tuke's 1858 *Selections* (1979). In his epistles to his friends Fox is seen at his best in pastoral mood, not battling against his opponents, as we so often see him in his *Journal*. As the epistles contain *ad hoc* expressions of points in Fox's teaching which are livelier, more intimate and loving than the more formalised statements in the *Journal*, I have been glad occasionally to draw upon them. As the extracts in both of these selections are brief I have referred to them by epistle number only. Tuke omitted numbering altogether so I have provided an appendix which gives the epistle numbers corresponding to his pages.

A reprint of the eight-volume American 1831 edition of Fox's *Works* has also become available recently. I have added some quotations from that fuller publication to remedy the deficiencies of the *Journal*. But the present work remains an aid to the reader of the Nickalls edition in accordance with my original intention.

I am indebted to the Danish Friend Elizabeth Holmgaard for awakening me to the fact that readers whose first language is not English do not realise that Fox's prose is virtually a fusion of biblical ideas expressed in the language of the versions of the Bible familiar to him. I am grateful to Mrs Gweneth Chambers for her careful typing of the first draft of the 'Concordance'; and to Godwin Arnold, Lewis Benson, Hugh McGregor Ross for reading earlier versions of the introductory sections; and especially to Michael Langford, John Punshon and Arthur Windsor for commenting on the Concordance; to my wife Else Pickvance for reading the whole MS and for her patience and encouragement in the years while this labour has been in progress and finally to Clifford Barnard and Sara Girkin for their care and skill in preparing this book for the press. Much as the text has benefited from comments and suggestions made by these friends and the care

1

taken to make it accurate, errors will inevitably have crept in and for these the responsibility is mine. I should be grateful to have my attention drawn to them.

JOSEPH PICKVANCE

Introduction

This Reader's Companion offers help of different kinds. To first-time readers of the *Journal* the introductory sections are likely to be of more value: to others who have read it from beginning to end without realising how deceptively condensed is George Fox's style of writing, the Concordance may open up more of the depths of his teaching. The method of theme analysis adopted here separates out the distinct ideas in his message and shows how they are connected. One feels that Fox only felt confident when reasoning by single, short logical steps, thus—'Christ is the Way'—'Christ is the Light'—'The Light is the Way'. Whatever the cause, this mode of thinking produced a solid framework of ideas which generates a feeling of solidity and strength.

Fox's prose may at first sight seem the work of a confused mind because of the unsystematic way in which he presents his teaching. My aim in the Companion is to demonstrate that his mind is clear and his use of language careful and consistent.

In the opening sections we see George Fox as a man against the background of the troubled times in which he lived; then as the writer of a religious classic. To help the reader with Fox's seventeenth century English, I have listed changes in some ordinary English words which he used, and supplied a glossary of specialised terms. A brief introduction to his characteristic religious vocabulary is given. Then follows a chronological outline of national events which are mentioned in the *Journal*.

The main part of the Companion is a Concordance to Fox's Christian teaching contained in the *Journal,* that is to say, to his interpretation of the apostolic message in the New Testament with which he gathered the first Friends in the mid-seventeenth century. The *Journal* does not give a systematic account of this teaching. Its main structure is a narrative of his preparation as a minister of the Gospel and of his travels in two continents. Doctrinal passages, and summaries of his three hour long addresses are inserted in the text in no particular order. The Concordance is not simply an Index, nor does it duplicate John Nickalls's index to people and places. Its method is to extract the main themes of Fox's faith and arrange the ideas of which they are composed in alphabetical order under characteristic words and phrases.

For Fox, doctrine and practice were inseparable; his faith and life are mutually explanatory. So, although neither the Nickalls edition nor consequently this Companion cover Fox's teaching comprehensively, the subjects included in the Concordance reveal much of the breadth and profundity of his mind and spirit and show how his spiritual insights found expression in practical living.

A work of this kind is inevitably subjective to a degree. The selection and exclusion of topics, whether conscious or unconscious, reflects the interests and comprehension of the compiler, as does the treatment given to them. I have included almost all references to suffering and sacrifices under 'cross', although that word may not always occur in the passages. This reflects my understanding of the importance to Fox of the *practice* of the cross in the everyday life of the Christian.

Elsewhere too the strict alphabetical sequence of key words yields to the rule of grouping related ideas, because the Concordance is not primarily an index or dictionary but rather a means of displaying on the page how Fox's teaching is composed of connected ideas. This method spares readers some of the labour of working through page references and of re-synthesising his teaching for themselves, while allowing them to form their own judgments.

In an ideal world dictionaries and concordances would be read from cover to cover like novels for the fascination of the histories of words: in our less than ideal existence I hope that readers will be tempted at least to browse in the following pages. If readers add to the Concordance references to passages that are specially useful or significant to them my objective will have been achieved.

George Fox:
'The man and his times'

Seventeenth-Century England

If the *Journal* is your first excursion into the history of this period, some words of introduction may be helpful. The reader who is unacquainted with the state of England during George Fox's lifetime is more likely to see him as an unsympathetic, rather aggressive character, and find it difficult to believe that he was in fact a revered and loved figure.

Certainly the impression that he gives of himself in the *Journal* is very different from that one receives from reading contemporary Quaker Journals and testimonies written by his friends after his death, unless one reads it with an understanding eye and close attention to detail.

The *Journal* is a seventeenth-century document and must be judged as such. Ways of thinking and behaving were very different then. Consequently the tendency has been to dismiss George Fox as a strange figure without relevance for today, and to accept Quaker practices inherited from his ministry without fully understanding the spiritual teaching on which they were originally grounded.

The mid-seventeenth century was a revolutionary period. In religion, the English people were deeply interested in the Christian faith, and much given to listening to public lectures and debates on theological issues, Bible in hand. It was a time of ferment in religion and politics. Sometimes the excitement spilled over into violence against opponents. Language used in speech and writing was vigorous to say the least. Some readers feel that Fox's language to his opponents was intemperate. But he must be judged by the manners of his time. Even the gently reared Margaret Fell addressed in print one obtuse Ranter as 'Thou poor blind sot!' Are the epithets attributed to Jesus himself intemperate? Also, the biblical overtones of some of the expressions used are not always understood: 'Thou beast' does not mean that the person addressed is no better than an animal, but that he

Quaker Cottage, Broughton Astley, Warwickshire.

Broughton Astley is a scattered settlement about ten miles east of Fenny Drayton. The cottage, which is represented above before modernisation, was the home of Edward Erbury in the 17th-century, and a meeting-place of Friends, with adjacent burial ground: Information from *Broughon Astley* by P. L. Jeanes (1974). The first convincements in Broughton were in 1647 (see p. 18/33–19/9). It is the earliest known surviving meeting-place of one of the groups which were established in the Midlands by Fox before his imprisonment in 1650. Another claimant for this distinction is Quaker House, formerly Skegby Meeting House, Nottinghamshire, reputed to be the home of Elizabeth Hooton (*c.* 1600–71/2, see p. 9 1646).

Drawing by Les Prince.

has shown which side he is on in the war between 'the Lamb and his saints' and 'the Beast' (*Rev.* 13-17), that is, in the war against evil.

In politics, the rise of the landed gentry against the autocratic rule of the Stuarts was reinforced for a time by 'the good old cause' of greater liberty for the common folk. The year 1659 was one of crisis and of disappointment of the latter group's hopes. That it was a year of strain for Fox is evident from the *Journal*. Theological and political issues were entangled: the section on social testimonies in the Concordance shows how for Fox Christian teaching and living made an impact upon the culture of the time.

George Fox the Man

Do not be repelled by seventeenth-century theological ideas which may today be rejected by many Christians or held in much modified forms. Theological fashions change, though not always for the better. The doctrine we now rather vaguely call **providence** (qv)[1] was held in extreme forms. All events being within the providence of God, misfortunes were regarded as punishments for wrong doing; good fortune was a blessing from the Almighty, a sign of divine approval and encouragement. Although best developed in the Old Testament, this view survives in the New Testament; the story of Ananias and Sapphira is a cautionary tale in this tradition. Individual cases, especially of random misfortune, have always presented problems. Jesus' creative response to the disciples in *John* 9:1-3 about the man born blind is significant.

But Fox accepted this doctrine wholeheartedly. He encouraged Friends to gather and record instances of **judgements** (qv) that befell some of their persecutors. It is not true, as some have assumed, that Fox got gleeful satisfaction from such reports. He desired the good of all people and he refused legal redress, even when justices urged him to avail himself of it, saying he would 'leave [his persecutor] to the Lord' to **forgive** (qv) or judge him as he willed (see p.415/22-25).[2] A wider reading of contemporary history places Fox and his followers in truer perspective and a more favourable light. Indeed the most important reason for reading about the early Friends is to learn why their ideas and conduct were, generally speaking, so outstandingly superior.

---

[1] (qv) and words in bold refer to entries in the Concordance below.

[2] Page numbers in parentheses refer to Nickalls's edition of the *Journal*: numbers following an oblique stroke refer to line numbers, thus: p.415/line numbers 22–25. Page nos. preceded by author refer to books listed in Appendices, p.144.

Perhaps the incident which troubles readers most is Fox's walking barefoot through the streets of Lichfield (p.71). I think it also puzzled him! It occurred shortly after he had spent a year in four Derby prisons, including six months 'in a lousy, stinking low place in the ground, without any bed'. The three spires of Lichfield Cathedral, like the sound of church bells, 'struck at his Life'. He reasoned with himself about the incident and later, perhaps much later, came across a possible explanation of his actions (p.72). We need to understand what stage he had reached in his spiritual journey, because a theological issue lay behind his behaviour on this occasion.

In the teeth of opposition from his fellow Christians, he believed that the power of God could be known in their day in the same ways and in the same measure as it had been in apostolic times. He sought to live under the guidance of the Spirit. The necessity of faithful obedience constantly recurs in his teaching. Three years earlier than the Lichfield incident he had suffered temporary blindness through denying immediate response out of prudent considerations (p.26). Later he was to remind Friends that, as everyone knew, some had made shipwreck of their faith through mistaking their inward guidance but that more had failed through disobedience. Nowadays we have swung to the opposite extreme. But now, as then, we walk the same spiritual tightrope on which Fox soon learned to preserve a remarkably healthy balance. We are in no position to pass judgement on him. We are perhaps more aware of how disturbing and destructive our deep-seated impulses can be than he was, so we should marvel the more at Fox's robust commonsense and general good judgement.

Interest has been expressed in the sources of Fox's income. He was bred in prosperous sheep country, and early showed competence in a country business. His living expenses were minimal. He ate little, though a 'bulky person' when Penn knew him in middle life. He economised by making himself a pair of leather breeches for horse-riding. In 1651 he had a good horse. He acquired an income early in life (p.50) from his own labours and possibly also from his mother's side of the family. His parents were not poor (see pp.60-61), bearing in mind that at this period a substantial farmer named Lago in a nearby village willed £100 to each of his daughters as dowries. Later Fox invested money in parts of ships or their cargoes. At his death he owned cash, a few acres at Swarthmoor, and 1200 acres in Pennsylvania given to him by William Penn. Also his testamentary papers refer to money left to him and his sisters by his mother in 1673 (pp.753-4). Fox signed away all his rights to his wife's property on their marriage—an action which some judges described as most unusual.

Physique
The portrait attributed to Lely corresponds with the descriptions of Fox's appearance. A woman observed that he was tall and big-boned. An order placed by his step-son Thomas Lower for a hat for him specified that it should be of the largest size. He was strong enough to separate two men who were fighting and hold them apart. Constitutionally he was fitted for the rigours of the life he was to lead. He could endure nights out of doors and could manage without sleep on occasions (p.151,160). He survived eight imprisonments totalling six years, often in unheated rooms and unhygienic conditions. Eventually his health was undermined.

His physical sufferings added to his difficulties. His handwriting, small and neat in 1650, subsequently became large and laboured, perhaps due to the effects of imprisonment in cold conditions on his fingers (pp.491, 510). Eventually his limb joints became so painful that he could not mount a horse.

Mind
Fox had great mental abilities. His early questionings took him from one divine to another (p.6) and from sect to sect (p.11). He heard lectures on biblical and theological issues given in churches and took part in the debates that followed (pp.47-48 Atherstone, p.122 Ulverston). Eventually he exercised the right to speak in church while it lasted (see **time (3)**). In the four years following 1643 he received an informal education that was perfect for his needs: his new synthesis of the Bible message was clarified and deepened, his views subjected to vigorous and informed criticism and his mind sharpened by controversy.

Probably his education was received at his mother's knee. He could read and write but had a form of word difficulty, such that his sentences were left unpunctuated; and his spelling might be termed random phonetic. 'Perils' was liable to become pereles, perrell, pearrell, pea-rall, or even, perhaps despairingly, 'per-'!

Thomas Ellwood chose to smooth the awkwardnesses of Fox's prose. Nickalls decided to re-introduce quaint expressions and dialect words, and leave untouched some passages that were not entirely clear. An example of the last occurs on p.547 where Fox describes a sleepless night during which he 'sees' 'tories' threatening him, (see p.547n) on the other side of the river. That this was a dream or vision becomes clear only in the next paragraph where 'the "tories" which [he] saw before' are identified by him with the English judges beyond the river Boyne in Drogheda who were an immediate threat to his liberty (cf. 549/2-3 'tory priests'). While dictating passages on subjects very familiar to him he had the natural tendency to omit words which the first-time hearer or reader needs for easy comprehension. But with a little patience the matter becomes clear, because he deals with such subjects again and again. William Penn said of Fox's public utterances that words sometimes fell from him 'abruptly and brokenly'. He was living proof that spiritual genius and scholastic ability are not insepar-able, and a standing encouragement to those who lack fluency with their mother tongue.

Fox's imagination was strongly visual. Ideas were sometimes repre-sented by physical images. For example, the danger of his own death was like a black coffin (p.573); impending dangers from enemies were like fierce dogs (p.100). Many other examples occur. Fox sometimes called these visions (p.539/1-540/3). The distinctions between his visual imagery and his discernment of coming events (p.487/15-28) or imminent situations, especially of impending danger (p.542/16-35), whether in waking 'visions' or sleeping **dreams** (qv), are impossible to draw. That dreams for Fox are a means of communication of God to man should be noted (p.9).

Perhaps through not realising Fox's cast of mind, many readers have found one passage about the state of England at the time incoherent and incomprehensible (p.575-6). Here is a very similar passage written by another deeply sensitive Englishman crying destruction also at a time of degeneration in the life of the nation: 'A man must identify himself with the criminal mob, sink his sense of truth and justice, and of human honour, and bay like some horrible unclean hound, bay with a loud sound from slavering, unclean jaws'.[3]

Contrary to the view commonly held today, Fox was a well-read man. Notice that he was familiar with the writings of Eusebius (p.495). He was abreast of the controversial literature of his day. *The Great Mystery* (1659) is a review of 108 anti-Quaker and other tracts. His private library included works by continental spiritual writers such as Jacob Boehme and Sebastian Franck. The 'Book of Martyrs', with which he was familiar, is *Acts and Monuments of the Christian Church* by John Foxe, a five million word history of the Church from the earliest times to 1563. So his oft repeated assertion that 'a dark night of apostasy' had fallen on the Church during the previous sixteen hundred years did not spring from ignorance of history or a belief that no-one worthy of the name of Christian had lived during that period— 'God has never left himself without witnesses', he said. He believed that the understanding of the nature of the true Church had been lost. Consequently the practices which properly belonged to that church had been replaced by others which sprang from false ideas.

Besides being a prolific pamphleteer he was a ready debater on religious issues with all who would face him, from learned theologians and political leaders, including the Lord Protector, to parish incumbents. His mind was neither academically nor philosophically inclined. He dismissed speculative, hypothetical ideas unrelated to practical living—'notions' as he called them. He refused to use theological jargon, insisting on keeping to what he called the 'sound words' of Scripture.

He had a great love of the **creation** (qv). He was a good judge of horses. Penn comments on his skill with sheep. Edward Bourne, a physician of Worcester, accompanied Fox thence to Tewkesbury and records that he discoursed on 'the language of the birds'. Was he perhaps the first if not the most notable of a long line of Quaker ornithologists? His interest in plants, particularly medicinal species, was lifelong. Thomas Lawson (1630-91), the well known Quaker botanist, wrote shortly before his death: 'Some years ago, George

---

[3] D. H. Lawrence, 'on the wave of criminal lust that rose and possessed England' from 1916 to 1919, *Kangaroo* (1923).

Fox, William Penn and others were concerned to purchase a piece of land near London for the use of a Garden School-house and a dwelling-house for the master, in which garden one or two or more of each sort of our English plants were to be planted, as also many outlandish (foreign) plants. My purpose was to write a book on these in Latin, so [that] as a boy had the description of these in book lessons and their virtues, he might see them growing in the garden or plantation, to gain knowledge of them. But persecutions and troubles obstructed the prosecution thereof, which the Master of Christ's College in Cambridge hearing of told me was a noble and honourable undertaking, which would fill the nation with philosophers'.[4] The idea of a school with botanical garden remained with Fox to the end of his days, but his project for Philadelphia (p.754) met with as little success.

He exhorted Friends to seek 'wisdom from God on [how] to use the creatures in their places to the glory of him who had created them', and he protested against the killing of animals for 'lust' (worldly pleasure). Finally, a modern sounding note, he wrote against the extermination of species: 'Leave all the creatures behind you as you found them, which God has given to all nations and generations'.

Personality

For estimates of Fox's character we must turn to the testimonies of those who knew him best. William Penn's Preface is one such, and should be read before starting on the *Journal* itself. Here are three shorter ones. Elizabeth Hooton (c.1600-71/72) of Skegby, the best known of the first women travelling ministers, looking back over twenty-five years of friendship, said of Fox that he was as upright and honest hearted a man as was in England. Stephen Hubbersty (1632-1711) of Underbarrow wrote, 'My soul loved him from the first. He was a father in Christ to me and to many thousands'. John Taylor (c.1637-1708) of Huntingdonshire gives more detail: 'When I first met

[4] Quoted in Isabel Ross's *Margaret Fell*, p.354. Philosophy then embraced natural science. Is there a hint here of the passion that inspired later Quaker gardeners in England and that was transplanted to America, to the Tyler Arboretum of Delaware County, and Peirce's Park, whose arboretum was incorporated in Longwood Gardens by the du Ponts, to mention but two in Pennsylvania?

him, he treated me in meekness like a lamb; he took me by the hand and said, Young man, this is the word of the Lord to thee: There are three scriptures thou must witness to be fulfilled; first, thou must be turned from "darkness to Light"; next, thou must come to "the knowledge of the glory of God"; and then thou must be "changed from glory to glory" '.[5]

Oxfordshire Friends testified as follows: 'He was a man greatly beloved; for all good people that truly feared God and loved Christ the Truth that were acquainted with him, loved him for the Truth's sake and had an honourable esteem of him. He was a man given up to serve the Lord, and to spend himself and be spent, endeavouring to promote the Truth'.

To show the high regard in which Fox was held by his friends, the story of Abia Trott will serve well. Elizabeth Trott (c.1628-68) was a wealthy young widow who owned a house in 'Pell Mell near James' House' in London, where a meeting continued through troubled years from 1660 until her death. She and her daughter Abiatha (Abia) were known to Fox and the Swarthmoor household, where Elizabeth's maid is referred to in 1657. Elizabeth, writing home from Barbados in 1662, says, 'Abia . . . doth often maike mention of thy kindness to her'. In her will, Elizabeth entrusted Abia to him. He, in discharging her trust, refused to allow the well-to-do John Drakes, also of Barbados, to marry Abia. Drakes, who by repute was 'a cruel swearer and a bad man', raged and threatened to have Fox burnt if he should come to the island.

Was George Fox universally admired and beloved in his lifetime as these testimonies might suggest? By no means. He had enemies at all levels of society and, as the pages of the *Journal* show, his life was often in jeopardy.

Thomas Ellwood (1639-1713), who knew him well, gives this balanced view: 'He was tender, compassionate and pitiful . . . to all that were under any sort of affliction, full of brotherly love and fatherly affection'; and he was 'a mild and gentle admonisher of such as were tender and sensible of their failings'. But, adds Ellwood, Fox was 'a severe reprover of hard and obstinate sinners'. Oxfordshire Friends

[5] The references are to *Acts* 26:18, *2 Cor.* 4:6 and *2 Cor* 3:18.

O frend you ar a magastrat in pla to

Fox:	O	frend	you	ar	a	magastrat		in	pla	to
Ellwood:		Friend	Thou art			set		in	place	to

Do iuests but imprisonein of my body you have

	do	iuests	but	imprisonein	of	my	body	you	have
	do	justice;	but,	in imprisoning		my	body,	thou	hast

Don contray to iueses according to your one low

don	contray	to	ieues	according	to	your	one	low
done	contray	to	justice,	according	to	your	one	law

O take head of pleasing men mor then god

O	take	head	of	pleasing	men	mor	then	god
Oh,	take	heed	of	pleasing	men	more	than	God.

said frankly: 'A terror he was to evil doers, and zealous he was in his testimony against deceit, to the end of his time; for which men, hypocrites and deceivers, hated him'. Certainly he was no respecter of persons. To an astonishing degree members of the social, religious, political and economic establishment feared his ideas, which threatened their dominance in society. The *Journal* tells how they illegally used the law courts to impoverish and imprison Friends and put them beyond the protection of the law.

Fox's seriousness as a boy characterised him throughout his life. He counselled Friends to avoid 'wild and light people' and to 'love gravity, soberness and wisdom' (Ep.1)[6]. His powers of leadership were recognised by soldiers (pp.64-65, 128-129) and men of religion (p.108) and women, whose service in the travelling ministry received equal recognition from the outset—they were the first to carry the message to the American colonies.

Of Fox's fearlessness there can be no doubt. He faced mobs, was beaten up on numerous occasions and was stoned while helpless in the stocks. He refused to return violence with violence. He led by example, encouraging Friends to face persecution while he went to where the danger was greatest (pp.560, 566).

As a public speaker, his voice had great carrying power, even in the open air, where, he said, several thousands were as many as he 'could well speak over'. Within doors, he could dominate a courtroom with its power (p.467).

Booted and spurred on horseback, with his long hair, searching gaze

---

Left: George Fox's Letter to Noah Bullock, Mayor of Derby, 1650.

This copy, retained by Fox, shows his small, neat handwriting of this early period; his erratic spelling and the absence of punctuation; and that by 1650 the testimony to the plain language—the use of 'thee' and 'thou' to all social ranks—had not developed. Thomas Ellwood wielded his editorial pen freely not only to 'improve' Fox's English, sometimes unnecessarily, but also to make the 'you's' conform to the later practice of the plain language, though not always consistently, see p. 55, 'I have no envy to you (*sic*) but love'.

[6] For abbreviations see p.50.

and powerful voice, he became a charismatic figure who could hold an audience for several hours at a stretch. He communicated to a Yorkshire throng the importance of waiting upon God in silence to receive power, without uttering a word (p.88). On this occasion his long silence spoke more powerfully than words could have done. 'He was a match for every service and occasion', said William Penn.

The Relevance of George Fox Today

George Fox has rightly been called the first of the moderns. He 'began again' in religion. Like the scientists studying nature in a new way at the same time, he set aside the traditional supreme authorities, in his case the Church and Bible. 'Experimental', or as we should say today, *experiential* truth, and in particular truth springing from a prophetic experience of God, was his touchstone: 'What canst *thou* say? . . . And what thou speakest, is it *inwardly* from God'?

It would be unreasonable to expect him to have freed his mind entirely from the limitations of his age. Certainly our view of nature has changed greatly since his day through the advance of science. Yet altering the way in which his message was expressed into a modern restatement does not invalidate his spiritual teaching because the human condition to which it was addressed remains unchanged.

We do well to remember that Fox was a villager speaking to villagers most of the time, with a full knowledge of their burdened lives: 'Take off oppression and set up justice over all', was his cry. We are still beleaguered by the problems which beset his generation: the spiritual yearnings, hopes, despairs, the need for healing of body, mind and spirit, social and class divisions, the oppression of people without work or land or adequate income, the destruction of the environment, bigotry and violence in religion, corruption in public and private life, greed for riches, lust for political power, the use of violence to further national, political, and economic aims, this was his world too. The essence of his Christian message is as relevant today as ever it was.

Fox's concentrated style of writing and his penetrating interpretation of the New Testament message call for the reader's close attention. But perseverance will be rewarded. Lives have been changed through acquaintance with this man whose jailers found him 'as stiff as a tree and pure as a bell'.

16

The Legacy of George Fox's Writings

To the serious student the sheer bulk of Fox's writings—the published ones which must be read in their various editions, and compared with the originals, which may be rare, and the unpublished papers, epistles and letters—is daunting. No one has yet claimed to have read them all. In order to understand the burning issues about which he wrote, a knowledge of the theological, political, economic and social thinking of the day must be acquired.

Several hundred pamphlets and one large publication, *The Great Mystery,* appeared in his lifetime. A long autobiographical work to 1675 became the basis of the 1694 edition of the *Journal,* and over four hundred epistles to Friends were printed in 1698. Other papers and epistles, including some of the best, remain unpublished. This remarkable literary achievement is largely due to the assistance Fox had from a succession of shorthand writers who accompanied him and to generations of editors who made his sentences presentable.

He had a strong sense of history, being of the stock of martyrs on his mother's side (p.1). No Lago martyr has been unearthed, but the descent may have been collateral. Lago suggests a continental origin *(lago,* Ital. lake). The earliest Lago records I have discovered come from London in the 1530's. Later, branches of the family settled in Buckinghamshire and the Leicester-Warwick border country. Lt. Col. Lago, the most prominent member of the family, bore the name Waldive, which had associations with Prestwich, near Manchester in Lancashire and Kingshurst in north Warwickshire. The suggested link between a cousin Bradford (p.3) and Robert Bradford of Manchester, the Marian martyr, has not been established. Fox's isolated excursion to Dukinfield and nearby Manchester in 1647 is certainly curious and tantalizing. His bond with the martyrs, whatever it was, remained a formative influence in his thinking (see **martyrs).** He knew he was making history and from his first imprisonment kept copies of the papers and epistles he despatched (p.54). Nearly forty years later he wrote, 'They will make a fine history.'

17

As spiritual autobiography Fox's *Journal* has won recognition. Ellwood's 1694 edition has long been acclaimed a religious classic. It is included in The English Library of classics in the English language, together with John Woolman's *Journal* and William Penn's *Some Fruits of Solitude*.

The discerning eye of Professor Sir Arthur Quiller-Couch selected the short passage on The Cloud on page 25, ('And one morning . . . the living God') for his *Oxford Book of English Literature* (1925). This is an example of Fox's simple narrative style. His prose, when it is not purely expository, is often poetical and lit up with flashes of inspiration. Even in the more solid of his tracts, the reader who quarries through the theological and biblical overburden will be rewarded with nuggets of spiritual gold.

But the finest passages are to be found in his unabridged epistles. Here, set out in verse form, are the opening lines of an epistle encouraging Friends during a time of severe persecution:

Sing and rejoice;
Ye children of the Day
And of the Light;
For the Lord is at work
In this thick night of darkness
That may be felt;
And Truth doth flourish
As the rose.

Only the *Journal* has been kept in print in Britain, so Fox's reputation has been determined by readers' reactions to it. These have been most diverse. At one extreme is Lord Macaulay's opinion that Fox was 'too much disordered for liberty, and not sufficiently disordered for Bedlam'. At the other is the view that George Fox was the greatest religious genius that the English nation has produced, and is still the least understood.

While Fox was alive, leading Friends split the Quaker movement from time to time over matters on which they disagreed with him. Years passed before some of these divisions were healed and his leadership was again acknowledged. Robert Barclay (1648–90), whose well-known *Apology* presented much of Fox's teaching in systematic form, omitted from it essential doctrines which presumably he did not think important. Thomas Ellwood, the principal editor, altered theological statements (qv under **'Theology'**: God and Christ) probably because they were grammatically or theologically unacceptable to him. Fortunately we have original texts against which checks can be made. Fox's most radical writings were excluded from the collected works, probably because they related to troubled times in the past. Toleration had now come and Friends were becoming more interested in the world of business. Fox's dying appeal to them not to neglect the preaching of the gospel went largely unheeded. They turned instead to the pioneering of the industrial revolution, and gradually became leaders of an important section of the new industrial middle class.

A few decades after his death in 1691 his teaching was neglected, and by 1750 the influence of a different Christian message with other emphases was dominant among Friends. This external influence was succeeded by others, the Evangelical Movement, and in the present century, liberal Protestantism. It is ironical that the forms and procedures—the structures as the sociologists of religion would call them—have changed less than the spiritual content of the faith of which they were originally the outward expression.

John Wilhelm Rowntree (1868–1905), the acknowledged leader of the younger generation at the turn of the century, began the first study of Fox's teaching. He 'believed that George Fox and the early Friends had initiated a renewal of primitive Christianity by re-discovering the Inward Light, the direct link from man to God . . . (His) vision was to use the history of the Society of Friends to demonstrate the relevance and modernity of its message, not just to his Quaker contemporaries but to the great mass of seekers outside the Society who were longing for a place of spiritual rest in an increasingly complex and bewildering modern world.' (Kennedy, p.38). More recent studies of Fox and his Christian message are listed in the Bibliography below.

How to read Fox's writings
When you pick up the *Journal* for the first time, skim through it to gain a general idea of its contents. Then read the autobiographical portions and narrative of events in more detail, without allowing the solid paragraphs of teaching to detain you—most of these are in the early chapters. You will find that Fox's life illustrates and explains his faith.

'Fox's classic . . . is nothing less than a summary of his total message given in anecdotal form' (Gwyn, p.93).

An important general point to grasp is that Fox's writings fall into the category of prophetic literature. This is doubly true: firstly, because he himself was a prophet of the Christian kind, and secondly, because most of his works are spoken prose. They were taken down by secretarial assistants (p.597 John Hull), sometimes in shorthand (p.340). He dictated the main parts of the *Journal* to Thomas Lower in 1675–6 during a rare period of leisure and recuperation at Swarthmoor Hall (p.vii).

The prophetic character of Fox's prose should determine how we read it: it should be read aloud. The meaning then becomes clearer. Probably this is partly the reason for the success of *Journal* reading groups: the Word of God has been heard through the hearing of Fox's words. That the words are charged with the Word may also explain the common experience that on later readings of the *Journal*, important, even key ideas, spring from the page which were missed during earlier ones. The Lord has opened the mind, as Fox would say, to receive more truth.

John Nickalls has reduced the size of typeface on pages 29–33, probably because he thought the text so condensed at this point that new readers might become discouraged and their interest might founder. Omit these pages at the first reading, but do not be misled by smaller type into thinking that they are of less importance. You will find that the reverse is true: Douglas Gwyn says of this passage, 'The statement bears careful reading to appreciate its immense implications' (Gwyn, p.95). But this can be left to a later perusal. We are dealing with a work that does not yield its deeper meanings on first acquaintance, much less to a casual reading. Articles on particular topics which draw upon Fox writings other than the *Journal* will also be found helpful at a later stage—see Bibliography.

Certainly the *Journal* is not what is called nowadays a 'fast read'. Fast-reading techniques should be forgotten and slow-reading ones acquired. Experiment with copying out important doctrinal passages. Look up the Bible references using the Concordance or a Bible concordance. You will find that each such exercise reveals a deeper dimension of meaning. Before reading a passage to a group, read it over to yourself until you feel you understand it.

In group study, an effective method is to copy out passages representative of core topics of the message onto large sheets of paper so that the whole group can read them, and discuss them point by point. Another way is to piece together the message from the shorter and longer summaries of Fox's public utterances given below, using the Concordance for expansions of each topic heading.

The Language of the Journal

We need to understand that Fox's religious language and his characteristic vocabulary are derived from the versions of the Bible that were available to him, especially the Authorised Version of 1611 and the approved Bible of 1568. Indeed the only language in which he thought and expressed himself was that of the Bible. The use of a Bible concordance on the first fourteen lines of page 277 will make this plain. For him, words had the meanings he thought they had in the Bible. And in only a few cases are his interpretations, though reasoned, improbable and unconvincing (see **nature (2)** 4. *Nimrod*).

Such was his esteem for the Scriptures that he normally refused to use other terms. Readers whose mother tongue is not English naturally do not recognise the familiar phrases that have entered the language from the 1611 version. Consequently they find reading the *Journal* much harder. It was to help them that I originally started on the present work. Although the Bible references in the Concordance are not exhaustive, I hope they will amply show Fox's dependence on it.

We need to be clear about this: there never was a 'Quaker' or 'Foxian' message apart from Fox's understanding of the early Christian message carried by the apostles which was published by 'the people of God' who called themselves 'the Children of Light' in the 1640's and who in 1650 acquired the nickname 'Quakers'. So what we are seeking in Fox's writings is the common source of the spiritual power of the first Christians and the first Quakers, which Fox claimed to have rediscovered.

First then we have to deal with the language of the Bible. Fox developed a fine sense of the meanings of Hebrew idioms. Anyone who imagines that words such as rest, peace, son, word, and mountain in the spiritual passages of the Bible mean what we ordinarily mean by them has not yet grasped that Hebrew psychology was basically different in important respects from our western modes of thought. And not only different but superior, giving a deeper understanding of the relationships of God to man and of both to nature. To draw attention to the more profound, spiritual meanings of important words I have used capitals more frequently than is customary nowadays,—thus, Peace, Rest, Word,—and have explained them in the Concordance. See also the section on Fox's Vocabulary p.26.

Fox draws upon the wealth of imagery in the Bible. Having exhausted metaphors from agriculture (the husbandman, vineyard, vine, sower), he may turn to the building trade (cornerstone, topstone, foundation, line and plumbline) and so on. His mind is full of ideas and masterly in its grasp of theological issues. So conversant is he with the Bible that he can express himself in so many ways that the problem at first is to discern the theme running through the variations, the inner ideas from the poetic expressions in which they are clothed.

Fox's special understanding of the Bible (see, for example, page 32, lines 1–4 and 19–29) gave him insights into the spiritual meanings of familiar terms and phrases. He confidently dispensed with the more superficial and literal ones. So he dared to discard the paraphernalia of Old Testament religion and of later Christianity. We find him preaching 'religionless Christianity' three centuries before Bonhoeffer familiarised us with the phrase. Similarly he saw the contradiction between 'There is . . . neither male nor female, for all are one in Christ Jesus' *(Gal.* 3:28) and the subjection of women in 1 *Tim.*2, so he rejected the latter in favour of men and women as equal or 'meet helps' in the order of the Church. Even today, Christians generally are not abreast of all his new insights.

Fox and the Spiritual Struggle Within
Like the apostle Paul in *Romans* chapters 7 and 8, Fox directs us to the continuous spiritual struggle within us between the forces of good and evil. This is a real conflict about life and death and is of cosmic significance. Today with the means to hand of extinguishing human life on our planet, we are better able to appreciate its wider implications.

The adversaries are variously called God, who is characterised by terms such as Creator, Life, Love, Light and Peace, on the one side, and the **Devil** (qv), or spirit of evil, death, disorder and destruction, on the other.

We have no choice but to take sides in this, 'the Lamb's war', (see p.341/10–13). Neutrality means assent to evil by default. This stark view of mankind's situation is biblical: 'See, I have set before thee this day, life and good, or death and evil . . . Therefore choose life' *(Deut.* 30:15–19) or, in Paul's words, 'to be carnally-minded is death; but to be spiritually-minded is Life and Peace' *(Rom.* 8:6). Reference should be made to p.17/21–23, 29–37 in the longer passage p.16/14–18/8 and to **Law (2)** in the Concordance.

Of his own early awareness of this inward conflict, Fox writes, 'I found there were two thirsts within me, the one after the **creatures** (qv) to have gotten help and strength, and the other after the Creator and his Son Jesus Christ'. Paul in similar state wrote, 'The evil that I would not, that I do'. At this time when he was beset by temptations, Fox sought 'the ground [root cause] of temptations and despair'. Then one day he heard a Voice say, 'There is One even Christ Jesus, that can speak to thy condition'.

The inward voice spoke to Fox's spiritual condition as powerfully as it had done to the apostle's on the road to Damascus and, as with Paul, the experience became central to his understanding and practice of the Christian faith. That the inward Christ plays a prophetic role in the relationship of God with men and women, both individually and corporately, is a doctrine, (technically called 'prophetic Christology') which was lost from Christianity until recovered by Fox (see **Prophet** and **prophet**). For him the voice of God and Christ is one: 'in hearing the Son, we hear the Father also, as the Scripture testifies' (qv), under **'Theology'**: God and Christ.

The commonest cause of misunderstanding of Fox's teaching today is a failure to realise how wide and deep and functional is the meaning that 'Christ' had for him. It is mistakenly assumed that Fox means what other Christians mean by Christ and his work. Not so, 'His Gospel teaching was intended to challenge the churches' teaching about Jesus Christ and how he 'saves' men' (Lewis Benson).

Fox states that 'the Spirit of Christ is the **Principle** (qv) of the

Quakers'. The Spirit of God and Christ is always present within each one of us exercising a prophet-like role. 'This is the Way, walk in it' *(Isa.*30:21). The 'Light in the **conscience**' (qv) that reveals evil is **Christ the Light** (qv) 'speaking' to us, teaching us the right(eous) way. It, not conscience, is 'the voice of God'. The 'Light' is the 'Voice'; our inadequate metaphors for describing communication between God and man fuse together here.

The early Christian movement was a fulfilment of Joel's prophecy that the Spirit of God would be poured out upon all men and women, regardless of age and class *(Joel* 2:28–9). The same could be said of the early Quaker movement, in which the desire expressed by Moses— 'Would to God all the Lord's people were prophets'—was realised to an astonishing degree.

So revolutionary is Fox's interpretation of the apostolic message, and so different his teaching from that of the Roman Catholic and Protestant churches that the warning needs to be repeated that he uses biblical terms with meanings which are frequently fundamentally different from those assigned to them in traditional theologies. The following is a list of some major points of divergence:

> baptism (inward and outward); true believing; beliefs (creeds); the Bible and the Word of God; the 'catholic' faith; the Church; the second coming; the cross; the inward cross; election (and reprobation); faith; the Gospel; justification; the way of the Light; the ministers of Christ; the 'offices' of Christ; church order; perfection (perfectibility); the power of God; propitiation; the inward resurrection; sacraments; sanctification; the Seed; the Spirit of God; the necessity of sacrifice and suffering; truth; social testimonies and witness; the role of women in the Church; worship in Spirit and in Truth.

Reference to each of these subjects in the Concordance will, I believe, justify the overall view that these differences are of a kind that makes all the difference, and that the early Quaker faith stands as a third form of Christianity. William Penn claimed that it was 'primitive Christianity revived', that is, the original Christian faith re-lived.

Bear in mind always that Fox's teaching is not 'mere' theology, that is to say, not simply intellectual philosophising about religion, but at almost all points is based upon religious experiences which are expressed outwardly in specific ways of individual and corporate living (see **social testimonies**). This is not to say that the reasoning powers are underrated in Fox's faith. Quite the contrary. Part of the cogency of his message derives from its intellectual coherence.

Fox and the Bible View of History

Earlier I have referred to Fox's sense of history. More needs to be said about a special aspect of this. Recent studies have increased our awareness of the extent to which he was committed to the prophetic view of history. He believed that the church in all its forms has apostasised from the state of the true Church in New Testament times (see **apostasy** and **night of the apostasy**). He gives a summary of the position in Britain (p.487). His message began with a declaration of the coming of the **Day of the Lord** (qv) *again—again* recurs frequently. The true Church is being restored *again* to its original spiritual glory (see **Fall**): the earth is to see *again* the resumption of the culmination of history in the end time (or eschaton), that the prophets had foreseen. Douglas Gwyn writes:

> Fox's message unfolds within the *eschaton*, the ultimate destiny of the world (in the Hebrew conception of it). Fox's entire outlook from spiritual experience, to the role of ministry and worship in the Church, to social and economic questions, is always involved in the cosmic drama of salvation history.

The Nickalls edition does not expound this view of history in detail, but significant references to it will be found throughout. Thus, Fox and Farnsworth warned people 'of the Day of the Lord that was coming upon them' (p.103); they are called to **repentance** (qv). Fox 'sounds the Day of the Lord on Pendle Hill' (p.104, see **sound(5)**); he senses the location of 'people in white raiment' which is the symbol of righteousness, *(Rev.3:1–6)*, and 'gathered' them on what John Punshon has pointed out was Whitsunday 1652 (p.104). On Firbank Fell before the crowd gathered he felt sent to 'sit down upon the rock on the mountain, even as Christ had done before' (p.106). He turned people 'to the Light of Christ that they might come to their salvation'. When he returned southwards in 1654 he had gathered 'a matter of seventy ministers' (CJ 1.141). The models here are the seventy elders of *Exodus* 24:9 and *Numbers* 11:16–17, and the seventy disciples sent out by Jesus (10:1–2). The exact number was uncertain; Fox also refers to 'over sixty'; George Taylor, writing to Margaret Fell in 1656, says 'three-score and ten was within the mark, for there were then seventy-three' BQ 155n.

It will be obvious, on this view, that Ernest Taylor's book title *The Valiant Sixty* is unbiblical and does not reflect Fox's purpose: it was actually an over cautious rounding down of a total of sixty-six. This new insight into the revolutionary Hebrew view of history is still too recent to have been fully appreciated (see also **types, figures and shadows,** Gwyn's fuller treatments and **War, the Lamb's).**

Fox's vocabulary

Fox had a simple terminology in which he expresses the biblical ideas at the heart of his teaching.

He used pairs of contrasting biblical terms to describe what we have to choose between, such as, 'the precious and the vile' *(Jer.*15:19). We have already noted life and death, good and evil. Some are made awkward by their archaic forms, for instance, the spiritual and the 'carnal' (fleshly, physical, worldly or unspiritual, according to context); the 'clean' or 'pure' are paired respectively with 'unclean' and 'filth' (1 *Cor.*4:13) (which sometimes means lasciviousness, but usually anything impure or defiling). A passage with other examples of such paired terms will be found on p.574/37–575/2.

Fox had a happy knack of finding rhyming pairs of contrasting terms, thus walking in the Light is opposed to merely talking of it; a profession of faith contrasts with the possession of Christ; and Jesus the peacemaker *(John* 16:33) is opposed to the Devil the peacebreaker, (but notice that Jesus disturbs the peace of the worldly).

When he emerged from his early period of spiritual turmoil he came to see 'in the eternal light and power . . . that all was done in and by Christ and how he conquers "the Devil and all his works" and is "atop of him" ' (p. 14). This struggle between the Spirit of God and the spirit of evil is described in terms likening it to a wrestling match in which we seek to conquer or triumph over evil. Prepositions such as those emphasised here are always important to Fox. Christ is *atop:* 'Triumph *above* the world! Be joyful *in* the Lord reigning *above* all the world, and *above* all things that draw *from* the Lord' (EJ p.41). 'Be valiant for the Truth upon earth. Tread and trample all that is contrary *under.*' (EJ p.212*). 'The apostle himself says, I keep my body *under* and bring it into subjection, I *Cor.*9:27' *(Doctr.*p.883). 'The pure and perfect **Law** (qv) of God is *over* the flesh, to keep it and its works, which are not perfect, *under*' (p.15). See also p.354/27–355/1.

Prepositions are so important to Fox that a second reading of a passage, giving greater emphasis to them, often brings out the forcefulness of this teaching. 'Be bold *in* the power of the Truth, treading, triumphing *over,* and tramping all deceit *under* foot, inward and outward. Having done it *in* yourselves in particular [i.e. individually] you have power *over* the world in general' (Ep.18).

Paired prepositions often appear in passages of spiritual counsel. Thus God and Devil are *within;* the **creatures** (qv) are *without* (i.e. outside); the Kingdom of God is *within*, fighters are not of Christ's kingdom, but are *without* Christ's kingdom' (p.357). Our spiritual 'home' or 'habitation' is within. Francis Howgill in a well-known passage says, 'Why gad you abroad . . . ? Return home to *within,*' and Fox counsels, 'The Light. . . calls your minds *within*' (p.309); 'keep (the) mind *in* [to God]' p.58; 'when your thoughts are *out, abroad,* then troubles move you' (Ep. 10). This spiritual advice requires a diligently practised inner discipline. Do not let the mind be 'drawn *out* by men, he says, because, 'Friends, when your minds go *forth from* the pure Spirit of God, and are drawn *out from* it, there the image (likeness) of God comes to be lost' (Ep. 32). The idea of movement towards and away from good and evil runs through all of Fox's thinking 'The Light will lead you *to* the Church of God, and *from* your teachers, to cease from men to be taught of God' *(Doctr.* p.3); 'False teachers are separated *from* the Spirit . . . and so *from* God, the Father of spirits' *(Doctr.* p. 99). *From* in such a context has the force of apart from separated from, or turned away from.

This teaching about the danger of becoming separated from the Spirit and about the necessity of keeping the mind within, waiting upon the Spirit of God before words are spoken or action taken, underlies Fox's description of Friends who received Truth and afterwards *ran out* from it. Any who do not wait upon their inward guide have 'running minds' (p.58/28). This expression is derived from *Jeremiah* 23, verse 21, 'I have not sent these prophets, yet they ran,' and was extended to all who were inwardly disobedient. So Fox warns, 'Take heed of forward minds, and of running out before your Guide, for that leads into looseness. Such plead for liberty, and run out in their wills' (Ep.83). His counsel to the Cleveland separatists who had 'tasted the power of God' but 'had not lived in that of which they spake' and had come to nothing, is an important illustration of this teaching (see p.79).

Fox attaches special meanings to certain ordinary English words which are theologically important or spiritually significant to him. As they may go unsuspected I append a list here of those included in the Concordance: **Abraham, animal nature in humans** (see **nature**), **answer, Bible(1), blood(1), clear(ness), condition(1), conscience, convince(1), divide, divination, experimentally, faith(1), fast(1), figures(1), fire,** fleeing 'in the **winter', generation, gospel(1)** and **(2), gospel order, imagination(1), inventions, Israel, justification, knowledge of God, low, measure, meat, mind, motions, mountains, naked(1), name, notions, offices, open, Peace(1), people, perfection, plants, possession/ profession, principle(2), profess, reach, religion(1), reprobation, rest, sacraments, salvation, sanctification, the sea(1), Seed(2)** and **(4), seedsmen, sons of God, sound(5), stars(3), summer, tender, God and Christ** (see under **'Theology'), Thing, time(3), translation, types, the Lamb's war, winter, world(1).**

Changes in the Meanings of Words

Since the seventeenth century, many English words have changed in meaning, some through loss, others through gain. Some of the alterations merely cause puzzlement—can it really be true that horses were fed on **meat** (qv) in Fox's day, and even baited with it?! But some were changes that were doctrinally significant. Thus, **convince** (qv) in Fox's time had two meanings of which the one that was more important to him theologically and the only one it has in the 1611 Bible is not that familiar to us today. **Experimentally** (qv) had not acquired the scientific overtones it now possesses. **Answering** (qv) now only implies responding, whereas it used also to mean doing whatever was appropriate to *evoke* a response: 'Be patterns, be examples, . . that your carriage and life may preach; then you will come to walk cheerfully over the world, *answering* that of God in every one . . . and make the Witness (i.e. Spirit) of God *to bless you.*' (Epistle from Launceston jail, p.262) The whole epistle should be read in order to feel the positiveness of the sense in which to answer is to minister.

Changes in meaning and special meanings are dealt with in the most appropriate places: biblical terms and Fox's special usages in the Concordance; and changes in ordinary English words in the Glossary, which also explains a few archaic and obsolete words, some dialect forms and a few legal and ecclesiastical terms. Reading through the Glossary, which supplements John Nickalls's footnotes, is the quickest way of avoiding misunderstanding of many details, some of which are of significance.

Recovering the Quaker Christian Message
We have referred to 'the message' of the early Quakers and to Fox's claim to have re-discovered the early Christian message. This concept requires clarification.

On this view the apostles in the New Testament and the travelling ministers of the Children of Light in the 17th century were *messengers*. They journeyed under a sense of God's call, of being *sent* as prophets with a message about the **Gospel** (qv), which is the power of God. It was a word from God, the **Word of Truth** (qv). It was an expression of an idea in the mind of God, instinct with creative power. It would be truer to say that the message carried the ministers. When this Word was sown by a true minister into the fertile ground of receptive hearts a fellowship was drawn together to meet in the power of God, that is, in the **Name** (qv) of God and Christ. A meeting of the true Church was established. Fox's first visit to Warwick in 1655 illustrates such an event (p.226). He 'had a meeting at a widow woman's house where many sober [i.e. serious] people came together. And a precious meeting we had in the Lord's power. And several were convinced, and stand to this day' [i.e. twenty years later].

So the secret of the rapid, almost explosive spread of the early Quaker movement and of its fellowship-forming power and its strong Christian witness was this message or teaching, which was short and could be learnt, practised, carried and published.

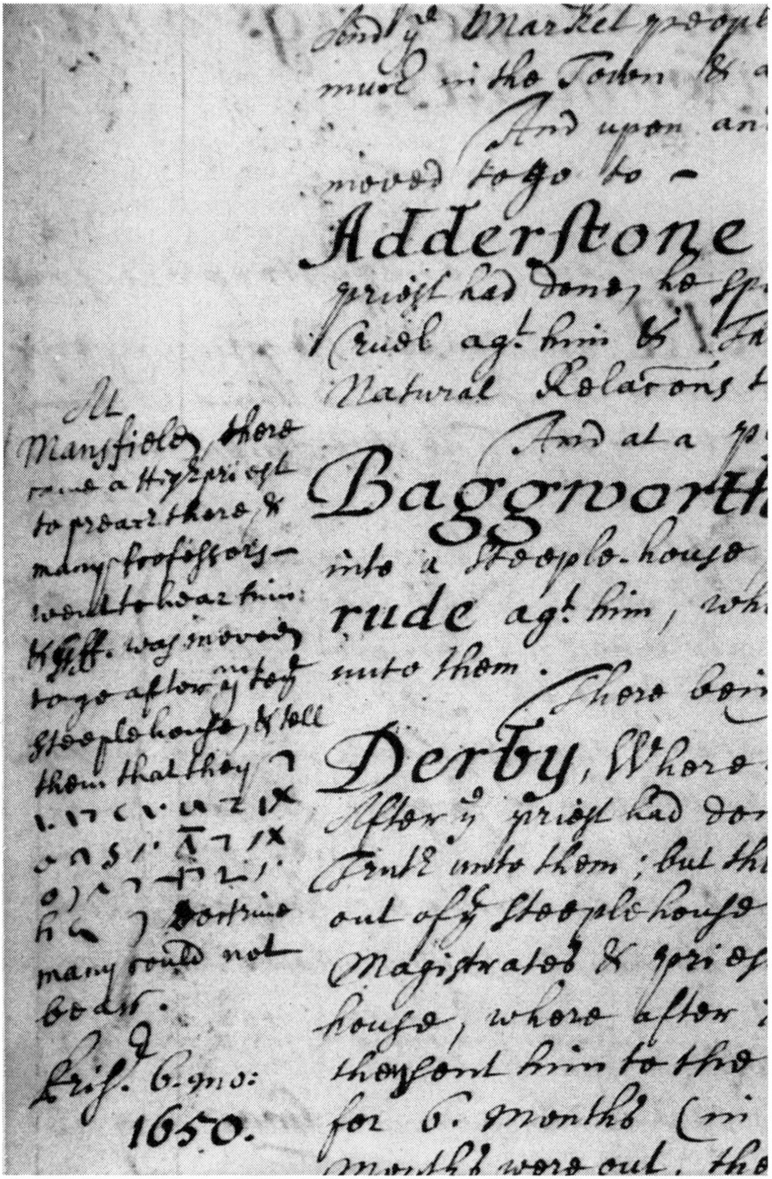
At Mansfield there came a Highpriest to preach there & many professors went to hear him: G.ff. was moved to go after ye priest to ye steeplehouse & tell them that they [illegible] doctrine many could not bear.

Trie'd 6. mo: 1650.

... ye Market people
much in the Towne & a
And upon an
moved to go to —
Adderstone
priest had done, he sp
Crude agt him & Th
Naturall Relations t
And at a p
Baggworth
into a steeple-house
rude agt him, wh
unto them. There bei
Derby, Where
After ye priest had don
Truth unto them; but th
out of ye steeplehouse
Magistrates & priest
house, where after
they sent him to the
for 6. monthes (ni
monthes were out, th

Nowhere in the *Journal* or his other works does Fox give a single orderly account of his long public utterances. He expects his readers to piece together the message. Scattered throughout the *Journal* are longer or shorter passages of detailed teaching, and also summaries of topics included in his fuller expositions.

Fox normally spoke for three hours, if not interrupted, when he

---

The Use of Shorthand by Seventeenth-Century Friends

A portion of *A Short Account of GF's Sufferings and Imprisonments* (Friends Ref. Lib., London, Portfolio 36,172). On the basis of internal evidence, Geoffrey F. Nuttall (*Bull. Friends Hist. Assoc.*, Vol 39, 1950) concludes that this document is a copy of a manuscript written or dictated by Fox soon after he was set at liberty from Carlisle prison in 1653. The handwriting he identifies as that of Mark Swanner who was for a time in the 1680s an assistant Recording Clerk. He regards it as 'an interesting fragment of early material in what may be called the *Journal*'s pre-history'. In it the order of places visited by Fox is not chronological and is different from that preferred by Ellwood from the *Short Journal*.

For information about 17th-century shorthand systems I am indebted to Douglas Lister, whose article in the *Journal of the Friends Historical Society*, Vol. 51, No. 3, (1967). p. 154ff, should be consulted for further details. His transcription of the marginal note, which is partly in shorthand, reads: 'At Mansfield there came a High priest to preach there & many professors went to hear him & G ff. was moved to go after them to ye steeplehouse, & tell them that they had no need of any man to teach them but as the anoint(ing) did teach them which they had received from the holy one which Doctrine many could not bear.' This should be compared with the longer version on page 20/4–19.

The shorthand is probably based upon Lawrence Steel's *Short Writing,* one of many 17th-century systems, of which at least six were used in contemporary records preserved by Friends. These records include original notes by Robert Barclay, and marginalia by Edward Haistwell. Not everything has been read, but no examples are known of Friends using shorthand in letters to one another. But copies of letters written by William Dewsbury, Margaret Fell, George Fox, Francis Howgill, Edward Cook and others, which are partly or entirely in shorthand, are extant, although the identity of the shorthand writers is uncertain.

The purpose of using shorthand appears not to have been secrecy, but speed in writing, and economy of space. Its most important use was by Fox's secretarial assistants, see page 20.

addressed new audiences (see 152/30 294/6 295/5). He frequently gives four-word summaries: 80/2 102/7–8 (Word not 'world') 107/7–8 157/11 210/36. Short summaries will be found on pages 91/30–32 92/18–28 94/20–22 121/11–18 122/12–14 150/5–7 154/3–7 158/5–11 167/23–25 273/6–13 304/18–29 305/16–23 319/30–34 330/28–331/2. Longer summaries or detailed accounts of topics: 109 (Firbank Fell), 152/12–31 (near Cockermouth), 155/3–20 (Brigham), 271/1–22 (Bristol), 272/20–273/13 (Tetbury), 283/13–35 (an epistle), 295/20–296/31 (Leominster).

As an alternative to reading the *Journal* and gradually piecing together the message, referring to the Concordance as necessary, the latter may be used by itself. Fox's own starting point was his common ground with the common people—our universal moral experience. Try starting with **Light(2)** and discover the relationship between Light and **conscience** by cross reference to **condemnation, inner** Light and **inward** Light, and draw together from **Light(1)(B)** what the Light *does* that is relevant to moral experience. Using the cross-references in this way brings out the tight linkage of Fox's ideas.

The Structure of the Journal. A Brief Outline

Chapter I pp.1–3 1624–43 Fox's boyhood and apprenticeship.
pp.3–9 1643–47 He leaves home and travels about, mainly in the Midlands.
Chapter I p.9–II p.39 1647–49 His spiritual search continues.
p.27 The Midlands—the birthplace of the Quaker movement.
'The Truth sprang up first (to us, as to be a people of God) in Leicestershire in 1644, and in Warwickshire in 1645, and in Nottinghamshire in 1646, and in Derbyshire in 1647, and in the adjacent counties in 1648, 1649, and 1650.' (p.709).
Chapter III pp.39–70 1649–50 Fox was imprisoned in Derby and Nottingham for about half this period.
Chapter IV p.70–VIII p.173 He travels to Yorkshire (1651), Lancashire and Westmorland (1652), Cumberland, Durham and Northumberland (1653).
Chapter VIII p.174 1654 The 'Valiant Seventy' (p.174/10–11) spread out over England and Scotland.

Chapters VIII p.174–XXV p.709 (1655–75) A narrative of Fox's travels in the public ministry in two continents.

summaries of his addresses at public meetings

epistles to Friends Meetings (p.58 etc.)

addresses and epistles to Friends in the public ministry (qv, under **ministry(3)**)

letters to Friends (p.282) and others (p.193 to Cromwell) and to 'the world' (p.203).

Interspersed in the narrative are shorter or longer passages for which Fox does not hesitate to use the word doctrine, though not in the sense of dogma. Much of this doctrinal material is in the first hundred pages, with the more extended portions in the first forty. Here one might have expected systematic presentation, but he prefers to speak of his spiritual journey and deal with his insights into truth in the order in which they came to him. These revelations or **openings** (qv) are fundamentals in his understanding and practice of the Christian faith. Gradually, during the four years when he 'dropped out' of ordinary life, they drew together in his mind and the message began to form. Once it was complete and had proved effectual, no changes of substance are discernible in it, but only a few minor changes of language.

Glossary

Legal and ecclesiastical terms, and English words with changed or special non-theological meanings Abbreviations see p.50

admire (at): v.t. to wonder (at); v.i. to wonder; n.admiration: wonderment (Obs.) 20/29; (a '14 day wonder') 229/8 352/29

adulterated: adj. corrupted, falsified 188/36–189/2

affect: v. to have a liking for (arch.) 601/27 cf. disaffected

after: prep. and adv. afterwards 58/23 132/8; according to Ep.45 7.55/23

alchemy: n. gold-like substance, e.g. brass (Obs) 201/29

alone: adj. only, sole, 603/17, unique, of itself, without anything more (Rare or Obs. OED) 302/7

amazement: n. bewilderment (Obs.) 74/12 see *maze* below

answer: v. to speak or behave in such a way as to evoke a desired or appropriate response; or to respond to such an act, etc. 263/2–9, 21–34; also, mutually responding or mutually agreeing 9/20–23

approving: refl.v., pr.p. to attest, manifest, give proof of 6.129/33

atonement: n. see also **atonement** and **reconciliation** in the Concordance
'None know the atonement of Christ but by the Light within' GM59/28 3.121/19

augmentations; n. increases in stipend obtained through action in the Court of Teinds, Scots law (OED) 207/24

bail: n. sum of money by which responsibility for the appearance of a prisoner is taken: forfeited if he does not appear 52/20 67/24

bailiff: n. officer of a court 226/14

bait(ing): v. taking a meal; or giving food, especially to horses, on a journey (OED) 87/7 541/8 546/8,16

blunder: n. disturbance (Obs. OED) 372.17

brave: adj. excellent, fine (admirable) 150/4

broiled: v. pa.t. to cause to become hot; fig. heated with excitement 146/4

bruit: v. to noise abroad (arch.) 61n1

bustle: n. disturbance 552/11

calendar: n. list of prisoners for trial 685/16

34

cattle (cattel EJ): n. farm livestock generally, not restricted to oxen 2/24

canting: n. insincere talk, pious platitudes (Collins) or perhaps the peculiar phraseology of a religious sect (OED) 690/31

ceil: v. to line, as with panels 383/30

close: n. an enclosed field 71/9 179/3

colour: n. pretext 326/30 563/32

comprehend: v. to grasp or understand Ep. 16; perhaps entrap (Obs. OED) 346/6 and thus overcome 544/4–5; to 'fathom', give victory over, subdue all that is contrary 175/37–42

concluded: v. pa.t. to confine, shut up in (Obs.) *Gal.*3:22 (1611) 11/23 see 21/14

condescend: v. 1. to deign 432/37;
2. to descend willingly and become at one with people (Obs.) *(Rom.* 12:16) 719/26

condition: n. social status 41/14 see also Concordance

confound: v. to confuse, fail to distinguish 9/8; to overthrow, defeat 372/24

conjurer: n. one who conjures spirits and claims to perform miracles by their aid (OED) 62/27; fortune teller 256/19,25,35

conversation: n. 'carriage and life' (259/36 263/30), way of living and behaving, see I *Pet.*1:15 (1611) 170/15 285/35 286/8 291/27 299/28 300/2, 7

convince: v. 1. to convict, accuse, prove guilty (the only meaning in the 1611 Bible and the more important and commoner meaning in Fox) 228/14,15;
2. to satisfy as to truth and error (Chamb.) 45/19 118/22, less certainly 19/9 60/29. 'Convincement' implies both meanings.

copyhold: n. tenure of land evidenced only by copy of court roll 355/24

coral: n. presumably red coral used for ornamental purposes 320/13

cover: n. excuse 83/21 107/31

cozen: v. to deceive 37/38

customary: adj. perfunctory or mechanical from habitual performance (Obs. OED) 341/21

cut off: v. spiritual sense, to cut off from the people of God *(Exod.* 12:15–22; *Psalms* 31:22) usual meaning to die 472/37 505/4

dazzled: adj. in mental confusion (Obs. OED) 44/33

discover: v. to uncover, reveal, expose 58/26 348/5

divers: adj. several, more than a few 27/13 cf. *several*

divination: n. foretelling the future by magical means (OED) 39/12–13

Easter reckonings: n. dues paid to the parson at Easter 207/24

elements: see Concordance

enlarge: v. to set free; enlargement: n. release 674/8

entail: n. legal, to restrict the descent of an estate to a designated line of heirs; fig. the necessary inheritance of sin from generation to generation 312/1-9

estate: n. state (Obs.) 6/2

faculty: n. the whole body (of Friends) (OED) 384/5 388/11, 17 389/35

fear: v. to revere, to stand in awe of (and obey) 204/31 see **fear of God**

flash(y): adj. probably splash(y) or marsh(y) 640/34 645/18 647/33

fond: adj. foolish or, stronger sense, imbecile 92/17

formalist: n. one who has the form of religion without the power (OED) 572/6

gainsay: v. to contradict 29/39

glister: v. to shine, sparkle, glitter (Chamb.) 219/2

groat: n. obsolete silver coin worth one sixtieth of £1 sterling 3/13 306/4

habeas corpus: n. legal requirement that the prisoner be produced in person and the reasons for detention stated. Based upon Magna Carta 1215; Habeas Corpus Act 1679, 384/27 681/23

holme: n. holly tree (Obs.) 127/26

hot: 'heats' in meetings: 44/34, see 623/5,6

hour-glass: see **time(3)**

impropriation: n. when the right of presenting someone to a church living is in the hands of a lay person 165/4 221/32

jakeshouse: n. an outhouse serving as a privy 477/3

jangling: v. to jangle, argue, quarrel 297/5

large(ly): adj. (adv.) full(y) (Obs.) 108/30; at large: in detail 341/38

lively: adj. living (Obs.) I *Pet.* 2:5 (1611)

mainprize: n. suretyship for the appearance of a prisoner 52/21 67/24

mandamus: n. writ or command from a higher court to a lower one 411/31

mark: n. an obsolete coin worth two-thirds of £1 sterling 249/28

mash: v. to mix, muddle 9/8 459/35

maze: v. to bewilder (OED); n. state of confusion 44/33 92/17; mazed: stunned 130/19; adv. mazedly 483/19 see *amazement*

means: n. financial income from church living or other *quarter* (qv) 81/33–37 223/35

meat: n. anything eaten as food, a meal, so not necessarily flesh 571/27; also fodder for animals 77/21 299/11 306/15 371/20; fig., spiritual food 193/27–29 see also Concordance

men-eaters: n. cannibals (of New England) 573/4 561/20; fig., men with the nature of cannibals 571/33 573/4,6

midsummer dues: n. dues paid to the parson at midsummer 207/24

mittimus: n. A warrant under the hand and seal of a justice of peace or other proper officer, directed to the keeper of a prison, ordering him to receive into custody and hold in safe-keeping, until delivered in due course of law, the person sent or specified in the warrant (OED). 52/8 55/12 671/1

moiled: v. pa.t. to wet, bedaub 352/26

moss: n. moor with peat (northern dialect) 127/28

moss-trooper: n. a freebooter or robber that once infested the Border area 162/1

mountebank: n. formerly a person who sold quack medicines in public places 38/6

mystical: adj. spiritual 585/13 'Is not mystical, spiritually?' 3.171

naked: 1. adj. unsheathed (sword) 49/20; without weapons or armour (soldiers) 255n; fig. defenceless (people) 255/34 366/7 371/6;
2. adj. going naked as a sign 372/32 407–8, 503/22–30 (signs, see *Isa* 8:18 and 20:2–4); naked usually meant without the outer garments or wearing sackcloth (407/35) but GF records that once William Simpson (see 407/30) went 'to Cambridge stark naked' (NPFG p.183). For contemporary usage, see Pepys' Diary 29 Jy 1667, 'a man, a Quaker, came naked through the Hall, only very civilly clothed about the loins to avoid scandal.';
3. spiritual meanings, see Concordance

noble: n. obsolete gold coin, one third of a pound sterling 455/5

noli prosequi: n. entry made upon court record when a prosecutor abandons a prosecution against a defendant (OED) 691/15

occasion: v. to afford ground, cause, or reason for an action (OED) 65/10 197/34–5; opportunities 608/25

original: 1. n. source, origin, originator 311/39;
   2. n. a person of marked individuality (Chamb.) p. xliii/16

own: v. to acknowledge, admit to, agree with 261/12; accept, have unity with 467/22–24, cf.disown

part: n. share in the ownership of a vessel or cargo 681/19

particulars: n. individual selves 336/21 341/36; individual items 341/37 400/29; adv. in particular: individually, see I *Cor.* 12:27 (1611) 173/20

passage: n. incident, event, happening 607/20; journey 612/6 cf. 90/29 91/15,25

plunge: v. to immerse: fig. to overcome by argument; overpower (OED) perhaps 'to sink' (coll.) 678/29

praemunire: n. sentence involving forfeiture of all movable goods and imprisonment for life 484/24 579/1–3 (MF) 487/4 489/4–18 490/22–25 (GF). The original law (1393) came later to be applied to any who denied the ecclesiastical supremacy of the Sovereign. Thus, John Punshon writes, 'It was in fact a fiction. Refusal to swear allegiance to the Sovereign was taken as conclusive evidence of another allegiance, the presumption of the statutes of Praemunire being that the other allegiance was to the Pope, hence a denial of the spiritual, and by extension (the fiction) *temporal* authority of the Sovereign.' Because of Friends' refusal to swear any oath their opponents could put them beyond the protection of the law under the statutes, despite their protestations of loyalty to the King (467/12–29) and denial of the Pope (475/3–5).

press money: n. money formerly received as signifying acceptance of service in army or navy 67/15

pretend: 1. v. to offer (Obs.) 383/20;
   2. v. to claim 28/31 cf. the Young Pretender;
   3. v. to intend, purpose 'If you pretend a warfare' *Doctr.* 1036

pretty: adj. fair, (fairly, quite) 441/1; (of people) of fine character, admirable 108/10

prime: adj. principal, most important (OED) 93/21

prove: v. to test (cf. probe) 'Prove yourselves, where you are' Ep.12 205/5: v. to give proof of 48/27–28, cf. *try, approving*

puddings: n. entrails 223/7

quality: n. persons of the upper social class or nobility (arch.) 215/7 *quarter:* n. presumably a church living or other office held: based on an interpretation of *Isa.* 56:11 (1611) 678/27

quick: adj. living (arch.) *(Acts* 10:42 *Heb* 4:12); quicken: (arch.) to make alive *(Eph.*2:1,5) 15/4

raw: adj. uncivilised, brutal (OED) 130/6

remove: v. to die 571/13 see 570/16–20

rid: v. to ride. pa.t. rode (dial.) 141/28, 522/11; rid of: rode on 101/22

riz: v. to rise, pa.t. rose (dial.) 102/7, 106/26

roar: n. a loud, deep cry of distress or pain *Job* 3:24, *Psalms* 22:1 (1611) 42/32,34

rude: adj. violent 358/4

rugged: adj. rough, harsh 416/24

several: adj. separate, different (cf. sever) 27/13 see *divers*; modern meaning, 226/11

slight: v. (of fortified buildings) to dismantle, demolish, render uninhabitable; fig. (of people, ideas, etc.) to disdain, show a lack of respect for 80/34, 94/11 230/21, 27 268/36 and 269/3 (GF and JN) 338/27 361/21 594/6

snew: v. to snow, pa.t. snowed (dial.) 648/13

sober: adj. serious (Fox's normal usage) 22/23 108/6 570/15

something (in show): adj. (people) of note or importance, *Gal.*6:3 (1611) 20/28

somewhat: adj. same as 'something in show' (qv) *Gal.* 6:3 (1611)

standard: n. flag or ensign serving as rallying point; fig. *(Isa.* 59:19 62:10) : 445/154 451/14 618/3; see also **Christ(4)**

staid: v. to stay. pa.t. stayed (arch. spelling) 106/2

stock: n. a fund 556/22; v. to put in the stocks (qv) 401/18

stocks: n. a device for holding a delinquent by the ankles, and sometimes also wrists (Chamb.) 44/28–34 224/24 (Evesham)

strange: v. to wonder at 126/31 270/21 336/25

substantial: adj. possessing 'substance', i.e. property, wealth; well-to-do, influential (OED) 232/5 259/30

term (of life): n. duration 697/7

throng(ed up): adj. crowded (dial.) 395/8 432/17

tipstaff: n. staff tipped with metal; sheriff's officer who carried it 682/26

touchstone: n. a test for gold, silver, etc., by their characteristic streak-mark, when rubbed on a special black stone; fig., criterion 40/5–8

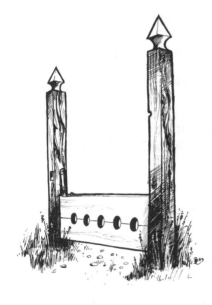

Village Stocks, Haveringland, Norfolk

Stocks were commonly used for punishing delinquents for minor offences. This is an unusually well-made example, with a rare, elaborate locking mechanism. Tall uprights sometimes had clamps for holding the wrists, but not in this specimen. In most, the uprights are short. The unusual structure at Evesham, described by Fox, p. 224/2–225/7, has not survived.

Drawing by Les Prince.

travail: n. bodily, mental or spiritual labour; often spelt 'travel' in 17th C. 570/10–14

traverse: v. legal term, to deny completely 469/18,22 183/32 691/2

try: v. to test 40/6 48/27–29, see also *prove,* and Outline of National Events 1654

wake: n. feast (dial.) 37/31

want(ing): v. to lack 199/26

wanton: see **social testimonies** (A)a(5)

watch: n. body of town guards 50/14 92/28 259/1–265/35; watch-bills a kind of battle-axe 91/23

which: pron. frequently used in 17th C. for who or whom 13/18

wildfire: n. a composition of inflammable materials (Chamb.) 353/8

writ: v. to write, pa.t. wrote (dial.) 61/132

An Outline of National Events 1624-1691

For much of the legal history, this outline draws upon William C. Braithwaite's article in *First Publishers of Truth* (1907) and on C. G. Crump's Introduction to *The History of the Life of Thomas Ellwood* (1899).

Laws enacted before 1625

St.27 Hen.8 c.20 Tithe-owners could proceed in the ecclesiastic court but this was not often adopted. They could levy a distress, the usual action, or begin an action in the Exchequer.

St.29 Eliz. c.6 Act of Uniformity and 35 Eliz. c.1 required attendance at church. Offenders were liable to a series of fines, and to arrest and imprisonment until they should conform. After three months imprisonment they were to abjure the realm or incur penalties of felony.

St.39 Eliz. c.4 This law 'against rogues, vagabonds and sturdy beggars' was invoked against Friends. The punishment was whipping of the upper body 'until his or her body be bloody', and a pass issued containing a description including distinguishing features, e.g. 'a man of middle statur of some thirty years of age, with brown curled haire' (Henry Fell, FPT) but see 42/11. An Act, passed in 1656, came into operation in 1657 extending the earlier one to 'all persons wandering without sufficient cause' (241/17 247 (mittimus), 258/29ff).

St.1 Mary c.6 By this Act persons were forbidden to interrupt the service or sermon. The malicious disturbance of a preacher in his sermon rendered the offender liable to three months imprisonment. See Nickalls's Index p.771 under 'interrupts sermons' (ignore the reference to p.76 but see instead 148/26-31).

The Commonwealth government enacted stringent laws against heretical statements which included Quaker propositions. During the Commonwealth until 1655 it was not unknown for persons other than the clergyman to speak after the sermon was over. See also **time (3)** and February 1655 below.

41

First Civil War 1642-6

1624 *July:* George Fox born at Fenny Drayton, Leicestershire (p.1).

1625 Charles I came to the throne of England.

1642 *August 22:* Charles raised his standard at Nottingham.

      August 28: The first action of the war was an attack on Caldecote House, Warwickshire, the home of William Purefoy (c.1580-1659), the regicide, who was a kinsman of the Purefeys of Fenny Drayton, which lies about one mile to the north of Caldecote. This is almost certainly the Colonel Purefoy mentioned on p.48 and not Major George Purefey of Drayton.

1643 *July:* the Westminster Assembly or Assembly of Divines, 150 clergy and laymen, appointed by the Long Parliament, met to settle the doctrine and government of the church of England. The great majority were presbyterians; eleven were independents (congregationalists). They were agreed about Calvinist doctrines, but not about church government. They sanctioned the Solemn League and Covenant with the Scots, binding themselves to introduce the presbyterian form of church government in England and Ireland in return for military assistance.

      September: Fox left home and began the four years of his spiritual search in the Midlands.

1644 *April:* The Assembly submitted the *Directory of Public Worship* to Parliament : it was ratified by both houses of Parliament. See 385/23-25 392/1-32 487/29-32.

      An ordinance forbade travelling on the Lord's Day without reasonable cause. Penalties: a fine or three hours in the stocks (224/23-5).

1646 The *Westminster Confession of Faith* was agreed. (The wording of the Quaker marriage vow is taken from this document).

      Charles I surrendered to the Scots.

1647 *January:* Charles was handed over to the English Parliament.

      October-November: The *Shorter* and *Larger Catechisms* agreed by the Assembly.

      November: The King escaped to the Isle of Wight.

Second Civil War 1648-9

1648 Parliament ratified the *Westminster Confession of Faith*.

      March: Royalist rebellion in Wales.

August: Scottish army defeated at Preston, Lancashire.

December: Colonel Pride's purge of the Long Parliament. He expelled the presbyterians, leaving the 'Rump' of fifty-three independents (congregationalists) who favoured toleration. The Rump Parliament set up a Commission to try the King.

1649 *January* 30: Charles I beheaded.

The Commonwealth

1649 *August:* Oliver Cromwell (1599-1658) landed in Ireland.

1650 *Summer:* Ireland subdued.

September: Cromwell defeated the Scots at Dunbar, Scotland (394/7). Penalties of the 1644 Act against travelling on Sundays, except for attending the service of God, were doubled.

Blasphemy Act: Against any person affirming himself or any other creature to be very God, or equal with God (134/28); or who affirmed that acts of gross immorality were indifferent or even positively religious; provided for committal to prison or house of correction for six months and, until a surety of good behaviour be given (51-52/27 61/2-8 64/34-65/18) for up to a year (70/17-25). For a second offence, the penalties were imprisonment until the Assizes (159/29-32 160/5 161/2-37 163/24-27) and if convicted there, of banishment under pain of death, (52/6 Derby; 133-137 Lancaster proceedings; 159-163 Carlisle).

1651 *January 1:* Prince Charles crowned king of Scotland.

September 3: Cromwell defeated the Scots at Worcester (63/8 64/22 67/11-22) Prince Charles took refuge on the continent.

October: Fox, released from prison in Derby, begins his journey northwards.

1653 *April:* The Long Parliament expelled 147/10-18 (inaccurate reference on 176/28).

July 4-December 12: The Little or Barebones Parliament (163n)

December: Under an Instrument of Government (226/28), Cromwell was given the title of Lord Protector with a Council of State to aid him. Oath of loyalty tendered to the army (176/7 176/28-177/7).

1654 Ordinance for the 'Trying' of Ministers: for the testing of their doctrinal soundness (295n); Fox's alternative test 206-207 207n.

1655 Fox suspected of plotting against the government (191/6). He was arrested in February (191n) and finally released in March (200/23).

February: The right of members of the congregation to speak 'after the priest was done' (see pp.24,26 etc.) was withdrawn. See *St.1 Mary c.6* above.

April: Proclamation of oath of abjuration of papal authority and of the doctrine of transubstantiation (220/15-221/20 220n 238/13-16). England divided into eleven local government areas under Major Generals (240n 265/8). Discontinued 1656.

1656 The Lord's Day Act was extended to cover persons 'profanely walking on the Lord's day'. It required attendance at church under a fine of 2s 6d and penalised any person causing a public disturbance of the minister with imprisonment and a fine of £5, or sending to a house of correction or workhouse for six months. See also under 1655.

1657 The Humble Petition and Advice offered the crown to Cromwell (289/12-26); Instrument of Government (308/18).

1658 *August 6:* Lady Claypole, Cromwell's favourite daughter died (346/7-348/16).

September 3: Oliver Cromwell died (350/28 350n).

Richard Cromwell proclaimed Protector (350/29).

1659 *April 22:* Richard Cromwell was forced by the army to dissolve Parliament.

August: Royalist rebellion under Sir George Booth suppressed (357/35-358/4).

December 26: The Rump Parliament sat again.

The Restoration of the Monarchy

1660 *February 3:* General Monk entered London (361/11 369/3-12).

April 4: Declaration of Breda: Charles promised 'liberty to tender consciences' (430/24 456/28 467/25 469/1-3 456/28). The newly elected Convention Parliament declared for the monarchy (354/20-23 369n).

April 22: General Lambert routed (372).

May 8: Charles proclaimed king of England.

May 25: Charles landed at Dover (375n).

May 29: Charles entered London.

700 Friends, imprisoned for 'contempt of court', were released (394/20).

1661 *January 6-9:* Insurrection of Fifth Monarchy Men in London (394/24 395n).

April 23: Charles II crowned king at Westminster.

Oaths of supremacy and allegiance denying the pope's authority and requiring allegiance to the king began to be put to Friends (see *3 James I c.4* above). Refusal was punishable by praemunire (see Glossary) (422/23 431/1 434/4 460/31-469/29 487/4 489/7 492/22 675/37-676/13).

1662 *May:* The Act of Uniformity enforced the Prayerbook on all ministers. Over 1,000 were ejected from their livings, including Nathaniel Stephens of Fenny Drayton, being unable to conform. This marked the rise of the English tradition of dissent and the establishment of Nonconformist churches: Presbyterian, Independent or Congregationalist, and Baptist, see 409/3-5.

St.13 & 14 Car.2 c.1 The Quaker Act was 'passed in May 1662 but had been taken in hand a year earlier'. It was directed against persons who refused oaths lawfully tendered to them, and against those meeting as Quakers away from their homes to the number of five or more. Penalties: first offence, fine of £5; second, £10. If distraint of goods was insufficient to furnish these sums, imprisonment for three or six months was imposed. On third conviction they were to abjure the realm, or be transported at the king's pleasure (430/24 438/34).

1663 The Kaber Rigg Plot in the north of England: an abortive Puritan plot (452 457-60).

1664 *St.16 Car.2 c.4* A Conventicle Act 'to prevent and suppress seditious conventicles' (secret meetings) was in force July 1664 to July 1667. It tightened up the provisions of the 1662 Act and introduced transportation for refusal to take a judicial oath (456/23 477/13 493/26-494/19).

1665 The plague of London.

1666 The fire of London (503/1-16).

1670 *St.22 Car.2 c.1* This Conventicle Act lightened the penalties of the 1664 Act, omitting imprisonment and transportation, but added fines for preaching and rewards for informers. Anyone attending a conventicle could be fined five shillings for the first offence; ten shillings for the second. The 'preacher' could be fined £20 for the first offence, £40 for the second, and if he could not be found, that amount could be levied on those present. The owner of the house where they met was fined £20 (558/29-35 560/19 561/18-564/34 566/18-20 572/15-33).

1672 *March:* Act of Indulgence: The King proclaimed the suspension of penal laws against Nonconformists and Popish recusants. Over 400 Friends were released from prison.

1673 *March:* Act of Indulgence rescinded. The Test Act: All office-holders were required to take the sacrament according to the Church of England and to repudiate the doctrine of transubstantiation.

1685 James II acceded to the throne.

1687 *March:* King James issued a General Pardon: releasing many Friends from prison (739).

April: Declaration of Indulgence: a declaration of liberty of conscience suspending penal statutes against Roman Catholics and dissenters (739).

1688 *November:* William of Orange landed at Torbay; James fled the kingdom.

1689 William and Mary proclaimed king and queen. Toleration Act for Nonconformists and Quaker Dissenters but not for Roman Catholics and anti-Trinitarians.

1691 George Fox died. He was buried in Bunhill Fields, London.

Annotated Word and Phrase List ('Concordance')

Aims

My principal aim is to shorten the labour of those who want to understand Fox's Christian faith, by unpacking the ideas with which his sentences are packed, and setting them out under subject headings to show how they are related in his mind. Thus you should be able to learn much from the Concordance before you check or expand your knowledge by using the references.

The limited objectives of the present work should be kept in mind. I have attempted simply to illustrate Fox's characteristic ideas and his typical vocabulary, and, where some readers may find it helpful, to explain or inform to the best of my knowledge. An exhaustive treatment would have been impossible in a reasonable space, and, with the limitations of this edition, pointless. Therefore single references indicate sufficiently clear examples, and not rarity of occurrence. I have drawn attention to rare usages and expressions that constantly feature in his writings.

Learning how to use the Concordance

Perhaps the quickest way of learning the method on which the material is organised is to refer to the three largest subjects, viz., **God, Christ** and **Light.** The first two of these have numerous sub-headings. Ultimately all subjects are analysed into single line entries, which illustrate distinct ideas and various typical ways in which Fox expresses them. By reflecting on these recurring words and phrases and the contexts in which they recur, their characteristic, and sometimes original and unique meanings gradually dawn on the mind, giving a sense that one is in the presence of a profound religious genius. Wherever possible I have explained Fox's meaning by quoting his own words. Sometimes a paraphrase or longer explanation has been necessary.

Subject Entries:

The subject entries consist of:

1. key words and phrases constantly used by Fox when expounding his teaching,

2. the social testimonies and witness of the first Friends, in a special section, and

3. some familiar quotations from the *Journal,* entered under a key-word, thus: **tree:** 'as stiff as a tree and pure as a bell'

Single Line Entries:

To help in this learning process the single line entries are often grouped thus:

(A) Statements which 'define' by saying what the subject is, or was, or has, or had; or is not, etc. For instance: 'The life in God is invisible'; 'the Church is not an old house'; 'God has a glorious presence'; 'the mountains (of sin) are within'.

(B) Statements which 'define' by saying what the subject *does* ('operational definitions'), eg. 'Jesus *opens* the Door of the Kingdom'; Love *begets* love'.

(C) Examples of Fox's spiritual counsel: eg. 'Mind the Light'; 'Wait upon God to feel his power'.

Bible References:

Bible references within parentheses immediately following subject headings are to passages which were important to Fox and they apply generally to Fox passages which are referred to or quoted in the single line-entries that follow.

Quotations:

Extracts within quotation marks are from Fox, rarely from the Bible. His actual words range from exact quotations from King James' Authorised Version (1611), to partial quotations or mere allusions. Where the connection is less clear, 'cf.' indicates a similarity of thought.

Page References and Cross References

'See especially' precedes page references which should all be read because they include some of the most important passages, either because they give clearer or fuller information, or because they are more comprehensive and illustrate the inter-connectedness of Fox's ideas, which is such a notable feature of his thinking, giving it coherence and solidity. Such passages are not always fully analysed in the single line entries that follow.

'See also' precedes subject cross-references and indicates where one or more additional single line references will be found. In a few cases, e.g. **justification, sanctification,** it is necessary to read all the information under the subjects referred to: this is because duplication of material has been avoided for reasons of economy.

Page and Line References:

References to the Nickalls editions of 1952 and 1975 are given thus: page/line e.g. page 144/line 14, 144/14. References not conforming to this pattern are to supplementary passages in other editions of the *Journal* or to material in Fox's other writings which are listed under Abbreviations below. In these the volume number is given before the page and line references, and where necessary the date of publication also, thus: (American edition, vol.) 8.9/42; (1698 edition of *Epistles*) Ep.262, p.297/40, or (Selections) Ep.20; NPGF, p.40/14. In each case the number following the oblique stroke is the line number

(+) and (−):

See **Light (2)** for a fuller explanation. The use of the metaphor Light is most appropriate when the inward Teacher reveals evil or darkness within us, that is, when it acts judgmentally or negatively. The Light also operates approvingly or positively, revealing what is true and good.

Line Finder:

The lines can be found quickly and accurately in the *Journal* with a book-marker down one edge of which is marked and numbered the line spacing of the larger typeface (see p.34) and down the opposite edge the spacing of the smaller type (see p.32). Line references as given take both into reckoning.

*   *   *

Abbreviations

adj. adjective

adv. adverb

Ann. Cat. *Annual Catalogue of George Fox's Papers 1694–97* H. J. Cadbury

arch. archaic

BJ Bicentenary Journal (1891)

BQ *Beginnings of Quakerism* by W.C. Braithwaite (1912)

C. century

c. circa

cf. compare

ch. chapter

Chamb. Chambers 20th Century Dictionary

CJ Cambridge edn. GF's Journal ed. N.Penney (1911)

Coll. Collins English Dictionary

coll. colloquial

dial. dialect

Doctr. Doctrinal Papers (1706); *Works* (1831) vols 4-6 by GF

EB Edward Burrough (1634-62)

EJ Thomas Ellwood's edition of GF's *Journal* (1694)

Ep. GF's *Epistles* (1698); *Works* (1831) vols. 7 and 8. Selections 1858, 1980

fig. figuratively

FH Francis Howgill (1618-68/9)

FPT *First Publishers of Truth* ed. N.Penney (1907)

GF George Fox (1624-91)

GM *The Great Mystery* (1659); Works (1831) vol.3 by GF

KJV (=AV) King James's Authorised Version (1611)

lit. literally

MF Margaret (Fell) Fox (1614-1702)

MM Monthly Meeting

n. noun

n footnote

naut. nautical

NB nota bene

NJ John Nickalls's edition of GF's *Journal,* 1952, 1975

NPGF *Narrative Papers of GF,* ed. H.J. Cadbury (1972)

NT New Testament

Obs. obsolete

OC Oliver Cromwell (1599-1658)

OED *Oxford English Dictionary*

OT Old Testament

pa.t. past tense

prob. probably

pron. pronoun

qv quod vide, which see

refl. reflexive

sing. singular

TT Thomas Taylor (1617-1681/2)

vi verb intransitive

vt verb transitive

Works (1831) Collected works of GF, American edition, 8 vols.

*   *   *

Abraham: the archetypal figure of a man of faith (ie. one who trusts in his inner guidance). He left tribe and culture, relying upon God's promise inwardly perceived. This inner obedience counted as righteousness (*Gen.* 11:31, 32 12:1-4 *Rom.* 4:1–22) see also **faith:** seed of Abraham: men and women of faith (*Gal.* 3:7) 336/8-10

access to God (*Eph.* 2:18); see also **faith; Peace, the first step; stillness:** true faith brings us to have 'access to God' 17/2 28/22 57/2 318/15 346/11–348/15 529/10

Adam to Moses: 31/12–23; see also **history of mankind**

Adam's states: see **state (1)** of Adam: the **Fall; history of mankind; perfection (1)**

addiction: 59/30-34 Ep.10 see also **temptations**

'alienation from God' = the **Fall** (qv)(see *Eph.* 4:18) 36/38; see also **sin;**

animal nature in man: 19/14–19 121/27–122/4; see also **nature**

animals: attitude to animals: 301/29–34; see also **creation; creatures**

Anointing: the Anointing to teach men (1 *Jn* 2:27): = the Light and Spirit of God and Christ 152/15–29; see also **Teacher, inward**

(B) the Anointing teaches within 8/28–30 20/8–10 teaches true believers 7/34

(C) mind the Anointing within you 59/3–7

answer: see Changes in the Meaning of Words, p.28; **that of God (1):** v. to act in such a way as to serve a specific purpose. Thus, a substitute for the correct key of a lock *answers* if it is effective in operating the bolt.

1. spiritual meaning: to minister by speaking, writing, or behaving (ie. one's witness, conduct, or way of living) in such a way that the Spirit of God in others is released from prison 263/2–12, 21–34

2. in weaker senses; to respond to, to correspond to, or be in agreement with 9/20–23 'answers the perfect Principle of God' 15/34–35

apostasy: the falling away ('defection'—Penn) from the apostles' faith by the Church as a whole in the post-apostolic period (see **night of the apostasy**). Fox describes this loss as from the apostles' 'doctrine, Power, Life and Spirit' (3.376) 'purity and practice' (418/20), 'Light' (8.75), 'true hope, true worship, true fellowship' (7.322); see also **Day (2):** see especially Ep.262, 10/34–11/1 100/20 339/16–24 342/

21–343/8

arm = power: 'the arm of the Lord' 44/1–16 'the arm of the flesh' 357/4

asking: the true asking, praying, hearing, waiting upon God, etc. is done in the true, invisible Spirit. The false asking, etc. is done in rebellion against and erring (wandering) from the true Spirit: 14/31–15/23 (15/12–19)

atonement: 'A great deal of confusion has been caused by the fact that the English word "atonement" has moved away from the sense it had when the Bible was translated, viz., "reconciliation" ' (Prof. D. M. Baillie, *God was in Christ,* Faber and Faber, London 1956). Fox could thus more easily avoid crude appeasement theories of atonement and **propitiation** (qv); see also Glossary; **justification; perfection; propitiation; ransom; sanctification;**

authority (in all meetings): is the power of God (= the **Gospel** qv) 514/6–14

backslider (*Jer.* 3:11–12): 'a sayer and not a doer' Ep. 20

baptism (1) = 'dipping or plunging' (*Doctr.* 682); see also **sacraments**

baptism (2): spiritual baptism (*Rom.* 6 *Col.* 2:12–13): the baptism in the heart; 'These things are to be found in man's heart' (16/17) 21/17–19 45/29–46/6; see also **ocean:**
one baptism and one Baptiser, Christ Jesus 210/14–15
with one Spirit into one Body (1 *Cor.* 12:13) 134/11–19 (Bible refs: Correct to *John* 6:25–58 1 *Cor.*10:16) 529/2–3

baptism (3): water baptism:
does not sanctify 51/20–21
John the Baptist and the apostles not baptised 46/3–6
infant baptism unscriptural 528/33–529/5
'sprinkling' to be abandoned 36/1–10

Baptist: John the Baptist (*John* 1):15/32–16/7; see also **baptism (3):**
'the baptism of John' 31/5–32/29

beast: the nature of the beast (cf. *Rev.*13:1–6): in a Ranter 81/10–23 see also **war (2)**

beget: to produce or generate (59/7); spiritual sense: to cause to be born (of the Spirit) through apostolic ministry (see 1 *Cor.* 4:15 *Philem.* 10): see **ministry (1)** (B); **Birth (2)**

Being (1); the supreme Being, God: 'the hidden unity in the eternal Being': how known 28/2–6

being (2): habitation, dwelling (17th C.) NFPG p.117

belief/believers: true belief/believers; see also **Anointing; haste:**

  (A) true belief stands only in the Light 16/7–10 34/16–19

      GF's 'secret belief stayed firm' 14/21–22

      believers 'are born of God' (1 *Jn* 5:1) 7/15–18

      are 'passed from death to Life' 7/16

      'are gathered into the Name of Jesus' 125/37–38

      'they needed no man to teach them' 7/32–35

  (C) believe in the Light 34/16–19

      seek the **'honour of God'** (qv) 37/3–5

Bible (1): = **Scriptures**: GF's understanding of the Bible; see also **Gospel; Light (1)** (B); **temple; Word (2)** (A); **words of God:**

  is the words of God, not the Word of God 145/28–32 146/8–10 159/26–28

  is not the **gospel** (qv) 445/26–35

  is not the **touchstone** (qv) for doctrines, controversies, etc. 40/5–21 687/23–39

  are to be applied inwardly (*Mt.*5) 31/12–31 (30/33–32/22) 45/31–46/2

  are known (only) by the Spirit (and Light of Christ Jesus) 32/2–4, 19–29 32/40–33/4 34/3–26 103/20–34 136/9–22 292/9–15

  scriptures were heard in the silence before they were given forth 359/33–360/18

  scriptures were given forth freely 39/8–10

  the Spirit and the letter of Scripture *are* separable 136/23–34

  the New Testament supersedes the Old 181/28–182/13 184/6–15 463/13–24 498/19–499/13

Bible (2): GF's use of the Bible; see also **history of mankind; social testimonies:**

  was 'very precious' to him 34/28 500/25–501/6 687/27–31

  had profound knowledge of it ('at his fingers' ends') 636/13–15 689/4–12

  speaks Bible in hand 112/4 196/14 326/22 (A. Parker) 352/32–353/2 431/31

  his preaching was an interpretation of Scripture 109 (Firbank) 134–135 295/21–296/31 303/7–28 316/29–317/18 342/33 345/33

  used only the 'sound words' of Scripture (cf. 2 *Tim.*1:13) 134/14

'birth'(1): the first birth (*Gen.* 27:1–32 *Heb.*12:16) 298/21 417/24–28

'the birth of the flesh' (*Gal.* 4:23) 311/9 561/8
Esau's birth 233/19 298/20–21
a person in the 'the first birth' 'lives by (relies upon) carnal (physical) weapons' *Doctr.* 675 5.400/30.
'Birth' (2): 'the second (new, or spiritual) birth'; see also **beget; elder; elect:**
is by the Word of God (1 *Pet.* 1:23) 24/11
the Birth of the Spirit 561/9
the new Birth 33/32–33 the noble Birth 311/37
the second (Jacob's) Birth (*Gen.* 27/1–32) 233/20–21 298/21
that no enchantment can prevail against 29/35–37
birth (3): the virgin birth 6/17–18 312/20
blasphemy: GF accused of blasphemy 159/29–32
Jesus accused of blasphemy (*Jn* 10:34) 203/10–29
Ranters 46/31–47/33.
'Blood' (1) = the Life of Christ:
(A) is within 23/16–18
is the 'Blood' of the new Covenant 23/16
is the 'Blood' of the Son of God 19/36; of Christ 23/11–17
is the Life of the Teacher who 'bought us' (1 *Cor.* 6:20) 154/6–7
is GF's life 19/29–38
is trampled upon by 'professors' 19/33
blood (2) = guilt or responsibility for bloodshed OED 98/9
blood (3) = life (in animals): Hebrew idea, see *Lev.* 17:11, 14 *Deut.* 12:23
'blot out' sins, iniquities (eg. *Ps.* 51:1, 9 *Acts* 3:19) see also **forgiveness; mercies of God:**
Fox normally speaks of the *blotting out* of sins by God, rather than of forgiveness, as though sin is erased, not only forgiven but forgotten (see *Jer.* 30:24)
body: 15/9–10; see also **circumcision; redemption**
Body of Christ: = the Church; see **church (2); baptism (2)**
'born again': see **'Birth'**: 'the second Birth'
bread and wine ('The Lord's supper'): see **sacraments.**
'Bread of Life', the (*Jn* 6:33–35): 'feeding upon' (449/22): = waiting upon the Lord in silence; see also **meeting (1)**
'bruising the head of the Serpent'(*Gen.* 3:15); the overcoming of sin;

see also **Devil; Serpent:**
Christ's power bruises the Serpent's head (=overcomes evil)
12/13–17
catholic faith ('catholic is universal' *Doctr.* 278): 529/6–23; see also
faith; Roman Catholicism:
works by love and purifies the heart 529/8–9
gives victory over sin 529/15
children of: fig. = offspring of, produced by, or having the quality or
character of:
(1) of darkness 60/6–1
(2) of the Day of Christ 29/15–2
(3) of Light (*Lk.* 16:8 *Jn* 12:36 *Eph.* 5:8 1 *Thess.* 5:5) 16/1–7 29/15–
21.
Christ (1) see also under the following topics:
Blood of Christ
Body of Christ
Christology (see under **'Theology'**)
Coming of the Christ
    1. OT predictions
    2. the outward coming
    3. the inward coming
    4. the second coming 'bodily, outwardly'
Cross (of (Jesus) Christ)
Day of Christ, the Lord, etc.
election in Christ
Fellowship in/with Christ
Generation of Christ
Hope
Jesus the Christ
Kingdom of Christ
Light (and Jesus/Christ)
Light (of God and Christ)
'Offices of Christ'
Power of Christ
Power of God (Christ, 1 *Cor.* 1:24)
prophecy (1)
Prophet (2), the (*Deut.* 18)

resurrection (1) and **(2)**
righteousness (3)
salvation
Spirit of Christ
Star, the (1)
State (2) in Christ Jesus
stature of Christ
Teacher (1) and **(2)**
'Theology'
Titles: see under **Christ (4)**
Truth
Voice of Christ
Wisdom of God.
Christ/Christ Jesus (2)

> **(A)**   is all 52/1–2
> is come 312/4–6 261/19–31
> is a Covenant of Light and Peace Ep. 292
> is the true spiritual food 38/31 (see also **meetings (1)**)
> is to be given all the glory 11/22–23
> is to have the best room, the heart 312/15–19
> is to have pre-eminence 11/25
> is to be heard 35/14–15 272/7–8
> is from heaven, his doctrine heavenly 484/17–18
> is the Life 14/20
> is the Life of the Teacher who 'bought us' (1 *Cor.* 6:20) 154/6–7
> is the Light, is God's righteousness *Doctr.* 96/49 4.126/9
> (that was crucified) is the Light of the world EJ 492/33–35 326/36
> is possessed 204/22–25
> is to be received (*Jn* 1:12) *in his Light* (NB) 327/1–2
> is revealed within 12/21 by his Light and Spirit 335/37–38
> is 'God's salvation to the ends of the earth' (*Acts* 13:47) 38/24
> is the Son of God 6/18–19 225/25–26 (*Rom.*1:3,9)
> is the free Teacher 258/28
> is the way to the Father 13/17–19 see also **Way**

is the 'new and living Way' (*Heb.*10:20) 35/9

is the Way to God 107/10–11 117/18 283/15

is the Wisdom of God (1 *Cor.*1:24) 38/37

is the Word of God (*Jn* 1:14 cf. 1 *Cor.* 10:4) 13/25

was the End (fulfilment) of all types, figures and shadows 367/9–18

(B)(+) see especially 14/8–30 34/3–27 34/38–35/19 261/19–31 367/7–368/4 368/24–38

abides in us 51/35

brings people through the ocean of darkness and death 21/9–12

brings people into the Truth 444/14

'bruises the head' (*Gen.* 3:15) of the Destroyer 13/25–28

commands his ministers to preach freely 39/10–13

converts 367/22

cuts off the entail of sin 212/1–6

destroys the Devil, the tempter, and his works 14/11–17 58/31–33 311/39–312/1–6 352/1–7 444/1–14

died for all 643/26

discovers (reveals) the roots of lusts, etc. 58/35

does all 14/11–20

enlightens every man and woman 11/25 29/16 115/16 326/36

ends all **types** (qv) figures, shadows, etc. 271/14–18 367/11–18

feeds people like a shepherd 272/8 the true shepherd 152/18–30

fits and qualifies ministers 7/18–29

gives: freely 39/15 Faith 11/26 Grace 11/26 12/16 Hope 12/20 right knowledge 38/37–38 his Light 12/16, 20 Power 11/26 12/16 his Spirit 12/16 Truth 272/24

judges the world by his Power 445/32–35

makes up the 'breach' (*Isa.* 58:12) between God and man 368/3–4

makes peace between God and man 303/28 367/28–368/4

opens the door of Light and Life 12/6

orders 364/35–36

overcomes temptation 12/13–17 21/37–38

oversees (as our Bishop) 272/8–9

perfects men and women 367/28–368/30

preserves 13/26

prophesies (= teaches) 235/15

redeems 367/15–27

reigns within 312/15

regenerates 367/22

renews into the image (= the likeness) of God and right-eousness and holiness 39/13–18 665/28–30

rules 312/15 400/14–25

saves people from their sins 117/12

shows a man his sin 64/12–13

speaks now by his Spirit from heaven 666/8–11

speaks to one's condition 11/19

spoke to the disciples and Jews 666/4–6

suffices in all deeps and weakness 12/19–25

takes away sin 51/33–34 64/12–13

teaches us to believe in his Light 312/12–14 318/5–11

teaches his people himself 107/9 118/33

teaches by his Power and Spirit 232/26–29 272/22–36

teaches like a prophet 235/15

teaches us in the silence 168/19–26

translates (qv) us 367/22

turns us from darkness to the Light 85/20.

(C) 'all is to be done in and by Christ' 14/13, 19–20 see **'offices' of Christ**

believe in Christ the Light (*Jn* 8:12,12:36) 16/3–8

'bring your deeds to the Light' (*Jn* 3:20, 21) 312/12–15

'hear him' 35/8–15 272/6–9

keep the mind in to the Lord Jesus Christ 30/13–19

'know Christ' 88/3 see **knowledge**

learn of Christ 150/1

'let him reign' 312/19–23

'look to him' 368/30

'mind him' 48/7–8 58/35

'receive him' (*Jn* 1:12) 368/30–33 in his Light 34/3–5

sit down in him 32/28 39/13–18

'stand in the faith' 58/33–35

turn to the Light 34/3.

Christ/Christ Jesus (3), the Word made flesh (*Jn* 1:14) 33/31 336/7

Christ (4): the names, titles, and 'offices' of Christ:

Although many of the entries below may be regarded as the work or **'Offices of Christ'** in the widest sense, Fox normally applies the term to the traditional three—Prophet, Priest and King—less often to Bishop, Shepherd and Counsellor, and occasionally to Commander, Orderer, Teacher and Saviour. The Nickalls edition is an inadequate source for the study of this important element in Fox's teaching. The following list is not exhaustive.

The second Adam 283/12

the Alpha (*Rev.*1:8,11) 163/5

the Anchor (*Heb.* 6:19) 14/22

the Author of faith (*Heb.*12:2) 318/12–19

the Beginning (*Rev.*1:8,11 *Col.*1:18) 163/5

the Bishop (1 *Pet.* 2:25)14/24

the Bread of Life (*Jn* 6:35) 18/16

the Bread from heaven (*Jn* 6.32) 294/15–16

the Cornerstone (*Eph.* 2:20) 312/24

the second Covenant 155/15

the Covenant of Light 38/23

the Day-star (2 *Pet.*1:19) 318/11

the Ending (*Rev.*1:8) 163/5

the Ensign (*Isa.*11:10,12) 618/3

the First (*Rev.* 1:17) 163/4–5

the Foundation (1 *Cor.* 3:11) 292/32

the Head of the Church (*Col.* 1:18) 35/12–13 174/22

the Hope (1 *Tim.*1:1) 12/20–21

the Just (*Acts* 3:14) 341/12

the Justifier (*Rom.* 3:26) 283/14

the Lamb (*Jn* 1:29) 341/12

the Last (*Rev.* 1:17) 368/32

the Life (*Jn* 14:6) 288/23

the Light (*Jn* 8:12) 283/13

the Lord (of Life) 312/16

the heavenly man 274/33 312/4

the spiritual man 274/32–33
the Mediator (*Heb.* 8:6 1 *Tim.* 2:5) 235/13
the Omega (*Rev.* 1:8,11) 163/6
the Opener of the door (*Lk.* 11:10 *Jn* 10:3 *Rev.* 3:7,8) 13/35–36
the Power (1 *Cor.*1:24) 96/10–14
the Priest (*Heb.* 9:11) 292/5
the Prophet (*Deut.*18:18 *Acts* 3:20–26) 235/15
the Redeemer (*Gal.* 3:13) 117/19 283/14
the Rock (1 *Cor.* 10:4) 288/23
the Rock of Ages 368/32
the Salvation (1 *Thess.* 59) 38/23–25
the Sanctifier (*Heb.* 2.11) 283/14
the Saviour (*Jn* 4:42) 35/33
the Seed (*Gal.* 3:16) 336/18–20
the Seed (=Son) of God 283/14
the Seed of the woman (*Gen.* 3:15) 13/27
the Shepherd (1 *Pet.* 2:25) 351/31
the Son (*Heb.*1:8) 666/8
the Son of God (*Mt.* 3:17) 167/12–22 666/1–3, 8
the Speaker from heaven (*Heb.* 1:1,2) 666/10,15
the Standard (cf. *Isa.* 59:19) 618/3
the Star of Jacob (*Num.* 24:17–19) 29/35
the morning Star (*Rev.* 22:16) 38/34–35 122/4 184/29–31 561/14–16
the Substance (of shadows, etc) 109/24 367/11–27 669/38
the Sun of righteousness (*Mal.* 4:2) 38/35
the Teacher (1 *Jn* 2:27) 288/23
the third Teacher 665/21–22
the Topstone 312/24
the Truth (*Jn* 14:6) 283/13
the Water of Life (*Jn* 4:14) 18/16
the Way (*Jn* 14:6) 226/1
the Wisdom of God (1 *Cor.* 1:24) 38/37
the Word of God (*Rev.* 19:13) 13/25 146/9–10
the Word of Wisdom (1 *Cor.* 1:24) 29/7–12
Christians: see also **believers; deceivers** (among Christians); **elect:** Christians in name only 417/21
church (1): the false church; 417/14–27 418/4–31; GF's 'comparison'

(= parable) 368/4–23; see also **night of the apostasy**

church (2): the true church (2 *Cor.* 6:16); see also **fellowship; tabernacle; Temple; wilderness; the Woman**

see especially 8/8–19 24/12–26 109/6–22 125/29–126/9, 10–19 283/19–35 444/27–29 500/3–501/6

is the believers 126/4–5

is the people who are 'members one of another' (*Eph.* 4:25) 283/20–21

is the people (whom God has purchased ...) 8/19 94/1–3

is in God (1 *Thess.* 1:1), the Father of our Lord Jesus Christ 24/27–28 35/11 283/19–28

is made up of living stones, living members 24/21–26

is the bodies of the people in whom Christ dwells 109/21–22 (*Eph.* 5:30)

is a spiritual household of which Christ is the Head 24/23–24 126/2–4

is the 'house of spiritual Israel' 13/6–7

is 'the general assembly written in heaven' (*Heb.* 12:23) 35/11

is 'the pillar and ground of Truth' (1 *Tim.* 3:15) 24/22

is Christ's 'Bride', 'Wife' (*Rev.* 21:9) 500/7, 'Spouse' 126/16

is 'the Lamb's Wife' (*Rev.* 21:9) 126/16

is 'the Woman' Ep.79 71/14 (1698) 7.89/36–38

is not a mixed multitude 24/24–25

is not an old house (of lime, stones and wood) 24/24–26 126/5–9

Church (3): church building: 'steeplehouse', a Puritan term; see also **temple:**

see especially 85/29–36 89/1–11 109/1–22 125/29–126/19 168/4–9

God does not 'dwell in 'temples' made with hands' (*Acts* 17:24) 8/8–19 40/11–12 76/5–7

men 'commanded' and made them 8/14–15

used to be called 'dreadful places and holy ground' 8/11–12

churches (4) (= Friends' Meetings): rare usage 174/4 177/8

circumcision of the flesh(*Gen.* 17:9–14) 38/20

circumcision of the heart by the Spirit (*Deut.* 10:16 30:6 *Rom.* 2:29):

he is a Jew that is one inward (*Rom.* 2:29) 114/30

puts off the body of sin (*Col.* 2:11) 38/28–33

civil authority (kingship) and the power of God (*Rom.* 13:1–7) 386/1–26

clear: to discharge a burden of prophetic service 285/18 447/38 554/1–2 706/30–31

clearness as to the rightness of a course of action 668/16 (hence 'clearness meetings')

colleges, theological 36/1–7

Comforter, the: see **Spirit of Truth**

coming of the Christ:
1. Old Testament predictions
   prophecies in *Daniel* chapters 2 (419/34–38) and 7:13–14; see also **son of man** prophecies in *Deuteronomy,* see also **Prophet (1)**
2. the outward coming
   Christ came 'above 1600 years' ago 419/32–33
   Christ came 'in the flesh' 464/21–23
   the temptations of Jesus 12/13–15
   the sufferings of Jesus 5/20–27
3. the inward coming
   is come and dwells and reigns in the heart 261/19–34 312/15–19
   is come freely 368/24
   is come and destroys evil 312/5–6
4. the second coming, 'bodily, outwardly'
   Fifth Monarchy Men 261/19–34 419/21–420/12
   Students of Fox are agreed that his whole emphasis is that the Christ came, and that he now comes within. He 'is come and coming to reign' so that some have come 'to sit together in heavenly places in Christ Jesus' (*Eph.* 2:6 8.182). This fact that the reign of Christ has begun gives him confidence that victory over evil will be accomplished. But Fox offers no speculations about a final judgement day associated with millennarian thinking.

commandment, the second (*Mk* 12:31) 29/1–7

condemnation (1) of the Light (*Jn* 3:19–21) 16/1–10 33/5–11 135/24–28
you must own (=acknowledge) your condemnation 144/7–9

condemnation (2): Moses' 'ministry of condemnation' (2 *Cor.* 3:7–9) 31/22–23 (31/12–32/29)

condemnations (3): by Friends of their own behaviour 269/7–11 (JN) 598/39–41 667/9 Book of Condemnations 511/18 (511/10–19)

condition (1): spiritual state: see **state (3)**

condition (2): social class 41/14

condition (3) that must be fulfilled; see also **growth**: 'None are converted to God . . . but as they come to the Light within' GM p.296

confusion and deceit discerned in the true Spirit 15/13–21

conscience: 'the Light . . . is not conscience' GM p.209/14 3.142/37; see also **Blood:**

the Light *in* the conscience 143/39 198/23–24

that of God *in* the conscience 188/10–11 222/2

'The Light shines *in* their hearts, and is not *there* the conscience?' GM p.13

'the mystery of Faith held in a pure conscience' (1 *Tim.* 3:9) 28/23

convert/conversion: 'from death to life, from darkness to Light': 283/16 367/32; cf. **redeem; translation; regeneration;** see also **condition (3)**

convict (= condemn) : (Lord Mayor) convicted them 563/26

convince (1) (=convict, accuse); cf. 'which of you convinces me of sin?' (*Jn* 8:46); see Glossary:

'be . . . still in the Light that convinces you' 283/40–41

'In that which convinced you, wait, that you may have that removed you are convinced of' 228/14–15

Double pun on two meanings of convince and world 484/13–18

convince (2): to be fully persuaded, lit., conquered, by argument 484/14

corruption(s) (*Rom.* 8:21) 12/7–9

counsel of God: (*Isa.* 30:1 *Acts* 20:27):

'None upon the earth hear the counsel of God or Christ's teaching, but they who are come to the Spirit of God within and to the Light within . . . And none hear the counsel of God, . . . but (unless) they come to feel it within'. 3.230/14–22 see especially 193/16–195/4

Covenant (1): the old or first Covenant (agreement) (*Gen.* 17:1–8 *Deut.* 27:9,10 28:1–68) 38/16–21 155/13–14 175/2

Jesus Christ the End (fulfilment) of the first Covenant 367/9–11

Covenant (2): the new or second Covenant (*Jer.* 31:31 *Mt.* 26:28 *Heb.* 8:6 12:24); see also **Blood:**

is Jesus Christ 38/23 155/15

is the Blood (=Life) of the New Covenant 23/16 (*Mk* 14:24)

is a Covenant of Life with God 2/15–16 441/16–17

is the Covenant of Light 38/23 174/29–175/5

is a Covenant of Peace 65/14–15

is 'the covenant of promise' (cf. *Eph.* 2:12) 117/15

covenant (3): the covenant in which the creatures are: see **creatures**

creation (=mankind (507/26–30), animals, plants, the sea, materials, weather . . .); see also **creatures; Providence; social testimonies:**
see especially 27/17–29/21
'gave another smell unto me' (27/19)
'things civil and useful in the creation' 520/8–10
'devouring the creation' 2/15–20 206/6–13
the redemption of the whole creation 15/7–10 see **redemption**
'all things are sanctified to me' 614/8–12, 16–24 614/33–615/3
'unity with the creation' 2/13–14 110/2–11 (John Story's pipe)

creatures (=animals, plants, materials); see also **creation:**
their covenant with God 2/7–20 (*Hos.*2:18)
are servants in their places 2/9–10, 'their right place' 60/12
their virtue and nature 27/24–29 28/15–19 29/7–12 287/28–30
use by physicians 28/15–19 29/7–12
use as food 2/7–10
treatment of animals 194/28–30 301/29–34 376/18–26

cross (1) =to oppose, thwart, frustrate 16/20–21 288/29 476/36 ordinary English usage

cross (2): a cross is that which 'crucifies' (i.e. slays, mortifies (=kills) inwardly, GF's spiritual meaning): 33/21–28; see also **crucify**

cross (3): the cross of Jesus (Calvary); see also **atonement:**
see especially 5/15–27 (*Mt.* 26:39) 63/6–24
bought men with his blood (=life) (1 *Cor.* 7:23) 154/5–7 665/34–35
'died for all men' (2 *Cor.* 5:15) 5/23 34/16–19 225/37
an offering for the sins of the whole world (1 *Jn* 2:2) 5/24–25
'tasted death' (*Heb.* 2:9) 425/10
'God has purchased us with his blood' 94/2–3 190/35–36
'Christ that was crucified . . . (is) the Light of the world . . .' EJ 492/32–35

cross (4) (physical): crosses of wood, stone, metal: their purpose 205/9–10
are needless 205/8–9
people to be brought off from them 36/1, 7–8 Ep.100

Cross (5) (spiritual): the inward Cross of Christ; see **power (3) of God:**

Annotated word and phrase list

see especially *Rom.* ch.6 *Gal.* 2:20 *Col.* 2: 1–14

(A) is the power of God (to save) (1 *Cor.* 1.18 *Rom.* 1:16) 174/24–30 205/6–10 283/7–9, 23–28 338/24 341/10–11

(B) crosses the (self-)will 365/30–32

'In *Gal.* 6:14, the apostle says, God forbid I should rejoice, but in the cross of our Lord Jesus Christ' 5.249/6–7 17/20–18/8

crucifies from Adam's state in the Fall 283/8–9

crucifies 'from' (EJ has 'to') the world 283/8–9, 200/10–22 (worldly honours)

crucifies from glorying in any but the true glorying 283/34–35

kills the (fleshly) self (*Gal.* 2:20) 14/36–15/3

mortifies (=kills) the deeds of the flesh 460/14–15 cf. 17/35

(C) 'Live in the cross of Christ and rejoice in it, which is the power of God' Ep. 216 7.218/33–34

if any lose the Power . . . they lose the Cross 341/10–11

(it) must not be denied 338/23–24

cross (6), the: daily Cross (= the power of God)

'Keep in the daily cross, the power of God' 18/6–8

'There is the true joy, the standing joy, in that which is from everlasting to everlasting' 7.173/40–41

cross (7), the: suffering through non-resistance; see also **social testimonies** (against use of violence) (A) (12):

see especially 406/37–407/26

acceptance of suffering 198/13–19 305/1–11 404/32–405/10 560/19–25 561/9–13

GF's physical sufferings 44/20–45/18

response to physical violence 374/6–13,16–21 376/11–17 404/34–405/3 410/1–35

cross (8), the: preparedness to suffer unto death (*Rom.* 12:1) 401/22–41 411/8–9 411/14–22 (Boston martyrs) 424/22–24 503/31–36

GF's readiness to die 49/16–23 198/5–12 227/5–22

cross (9): suffering and rejoicing: see also **patience**

'Sing and rejoice . . . ' (under persecution) Ep. 227

through obedience (2 *Cor.*1:12) 401/3–33 406/10–13

through testimonies 37/5–20 169/20–25 494/25–38 560/5–16

for righteousness' sake 424/19–27 574/26–575/3

cross (10), the: suffering for one's brother and sister: 42/3–5(1649) 221/27–222/3 349/14–23 383/8 (MF)

cross (11), the: suffering in the will of God: 5/17–19 53/11–20 54/14–16 67/28–33 670/11–13 681/1–10 EJ 491/16–28

cross (12), the: sufferings spread the message: 157/19–31 (Carlisle) 254/ 18–255/6 (Launceston) 259/11–22 401/3–9 424/1–30 (Derby)

Cross (13), the: fellowship in the Cross (= the power of God) (= 'mystery' : Greek sense, a secret revealed to the initiated):

in which mystery of the Cross is the Fellowship (*Eph.* 3:1–9) 283/ 32–35

'He that has fellowship with him [Christ] in his sufferings, shall have fellowship with him in his glory' 7.56/17–18

Crown: the Crown of glory (1 *Pet.* 5.4 1 *Cor.* 9:25)

the crown 'that fades not away' 198/12–19

if any lose the Power, they lose their Crown 341/10–12

crucify: fig. spiritual sense, to kill, slay (*Heb.* 6:6) see also **cross (2), (3), (5)**: 'the powers . . . were crucifying the Seed, Christ, in themselves and others' 354/9–12 341/10–13

darkness: = evil, wickedness, iniquity; see also **death** ('ocean of . . .'):

GF senses an evil power 542/18, 24–30 548/25–26

power of darkness 548/25–26

darkness to Light 27/10–12 34/3–6 89/13–16

'children of darkness' 60/6–10 see also **children of**

Day (1) (of Christ, the Lord etc.):

of Christ 29/15–21 271/19–21 666/9–11 669/35–36

of darkness (see 'day of recompense' below) 349/30–31

of God 115/32–33 (and 'sons of God') 167/12–22

Gospel Day, this 666/11

Lamb's day, this 163/3

of the Lord (most frequent form) 36/22–26 51/11–12 121/13 316/ 13–15 393/9–19

of judgement 320/23 576/12–24 judgements 393/19 see also **Day (3)**

of recompense (= day of darkness) 361/20 (393/9–10,19)

of salvation 94/21

of visitation 94/21 290/10–11 338/25–30

Day (2) (of Christ, the Lord, etc.)

(A) is everlasting 152/12

is 'great and terrible' (*Joel* 2:11) 38/3–4

is heavenly 36/24

'is come and coming' 236/31 55/23–27 (1650) (cf. *Rev.* 1:4,19 4:8)

'was coming upon all evil doers' 300/22 333/5–6 and 'deceitful ways, doings and merchandize' 121/13–18 157/2–3

comes upon 'all sin and wickedness' 304/26–29 305/17–18 326/27–28

and upon 'all ungodliness and unrighteousness' 90/34

'was come' and the night of apostasy ended 155/13–18

'was coming' (future) 121/18

'came upon them' 393/10

'has sprung from on high' 36/24–25 669/36

'was springing from on high' (now) 271/20

declared 120/1 201/15–16 321/3

preached 305/17

proclaimed 115/33 and set over all 223/33

sounded amongst them 299/7–8 see also **sound**

(people) warned of 97/29 234/25 238/25 393/4–10

(B) 'broke forth apace' 36/25

dawns in the heart (2 *Pet.* 1:19) 40/4

shines 362/1–2

'all hearts shall be manifest; the secrets of everyone's heart shall be revealed by the Light . . . which comes from Jesus Christ' 236/31–34

'in his Day all things are seen, visible and invisible, by the divine Light of Christ' 29/18–19

Friends were 'redeemed out of [holy] days and brought into his Day' 669/34–37

days: holy days and the Day 669/27–38; see also **social testimonies**(B) (5)

Day–star, the (=Christ) (2 *Pet.* 1:17–19): arises in the heart 40/1–5

death (see *Rom.* 5:12–21 and 6:1–23); see also **darkness**:

death and darkness in people 49/3–5

ocean of darkness and death 19/24–28 21/10–11

'the law of sin and death' (*Rom.* 8:2) 38/28

was/is brought by sin (*Rom.* 5:12) 31/23

fleshly knowledge works death (cf. 1 *Pet.* 2:11) 10/30–31

comes of going forth into the creatures and visible things 60/14–16 'oppressed the Seed of God in man' 13/36–38

'passed upon all men' (*Rom.* 5:12) 13/37

the elect seed of God (Quakers) where 'death is brought into the death' 281/3–4

deceit: the deceit (*Psalms* 101:7): see also **social testimonies** (A) (1) (deceitful merchandise etc):

'priests' stand in the deceit 29/22–23

'the deceit of the heart' (*Prov.* 12:20 *Jer.* 17:9) 135/26

is worked down by the Spirit 354/33–34

deceivers: the greatest deceivers:

among the Jews 29/26–30/1

among the Christians (those who) 'could speak some experiences of Christ and God but lived not in the Life' 30/1–19

cannot deceive the elect 30/15

despair: also 'melancholy' (probably, depression); see also **temptations:** By 'I was tempted almost to despair' (4/15), Fox meant that he was tempted at this time (1644) to take his own life. In 1653 he wrote 'You that have been in the wilderness, *can witness with me,* and the same temptations, even to despair and *to make away with themselves'.* Ep. 45 7.55/26–28. Benson gives other contemporary instances of this use of 'to make away with'. This experience was 'the depths of Satan' (34/35), 4/4–23 5/36 6/14 12/9–25 14/26–30

Destroyer, the: 13/22–28 see also the **Devil**

Devil (1); the (*Gen.* 3:1, *Rev.* 12:9, 20:2); see also **Christ (2) (B); Destroyer; evil; prince of darkness; Serpent; Tempter:**

see especially 212/26–36 443/25–444/14 665/16–26

(A) is the 'original' (originator) of sin 311/39–312/9

is 'the power of darkness' 542/27–28

is the prince of darkness 16/7–10

is the false teacher and the head of all false teachers 665/24–26

is 'the second teacher' 665/17–18

is 'the evil spirit' 542/17–543/1

is a 'liar and murderer' 212/26–36

is overcome by Christ 12/13–15

was not made by God 212/26–31

was first a serpent, then a devil and adversary; then the Devil became a destroyer, then a dragon (*Rev.* 20:2) 443/36–444/5

(B) cannot comprehend the Light (*Jn* 1:5) 544/4–5

draws people out of Truth into condemnation 16/9–10

went out of Truth 212/30

Devil (2): 'of the Devil': those who 'went out of the Truth' 444/2–4

discernment: spiritual discernment: of people's states and conditions (155/27–35) 14/33–15/25

discipline: within the fellowship: see **condemnations (3)**

disobedience: to the Light 135/24–28 144/5–12

the 'fleshly mind, spirit, will, which lives in disobedience' 16/20–23

divide the word: divide *to* or *among:* to minister in words appropriately, including preaching, to different groups: 125/22–23; see also **minister (1) (B)**

divination: foretelling the future by magical means (OED) 39/12–13

dominion: government, authority over: the power of God had great dominion 545/24

Door, the: the spiritual door in the heart (*Jn* 10:1–9) 'The Light is the Door' *Doctr.* 101/40 4.132/24

of Light and Life 12/6 (*Jn* 8:12)

Jesus the Opener 13/35–36 see **Christ (4)**

dreams: kinds of dreams: 9/5–13 see p.10 above

drinking: see eating

earth, the = 'earthly nature', contrasted with the heavenly; see also **flesh; ground (2); plough; Seed (5); woman:**

is in men's hearts 22/7 331/26

is hypocrisy, falseness 331/26–27

is the 'rough', 'crooked' and 'mountainous' (*Lk.* 3:5) 16/14–19

is 'like fallow ground' 39/30–31

is to be cracked and shaken 22/3–10

earthly, the (contrasted with heavenly) (*Jn* 3:31): the *changeable* ways, religions, things, creatures and teachers 13/11–20

eating and drinking; see **lusts; social testimonies** (A) (14)

education:

training children and servants in the new Covenant 38/21–28 instruction in things civil and useful in the creation 520/10

elder, the; the elder (son) (*Rom.* 9:9–13); see also **'birth' (1); 'Birth'(2):**

is servant to the younger 281/4

is 'the first birth' Esau: (Jacob, the younger is 'the second birth') 298/21

elect/election and reprobation: see also **reprobation**:

GF has a doctrine 157/28–29 298/10–11

GF argues against Calvinists' doctrine 316/16–317/31–318/19 550/1–18

GF argues against Baptists' doctrine of particular (individual) election 233/16-26

the elect are born again 233/21–22

the elect 'obtain the promise' 175/16 233/14–26

the election stands in the second Birth, reprobation in the first 86/22–30 see also **birth (1)** and **(2)**

the elect must walk in the Light, etc. 233/24–25 see also **justification**

belief in the Light brings salvation, and hating it, condemnation (=reprobation) 175/6–13 317/10–12 550/14–16)

election and choice stand in Christ (*Gal.* 3:16) 550/14–16

the elect are impossible to deceive (*Mt.* 24:24) 30/14–16

Quakers, the elect seed of God 281/3–4 see also **Quakers**

element/elements: (1) 'my holy element'; sphere of work 720/32

(2) perhaps earth, air, fire, water (the components of the natural world according to ancient philosophies), or the heavenly bodies (cf. 2 *Pet.* 3:10,12) 25/18

(3) elements (*Gal.* 4:9) the bread and wine in the Lord's Supper or Communion Service; and water in the baptismal service:

'outward elementary things' *Doctr.* 935/1–10 6.283/40–284/5

'Cannot *reprobates* be sprinkled with the elements of water and take the elements of bread and wine?' *Doctr.* 935/48–49 6.285/1–2

(4) probably the sky, the upper atmosphere, 'heaven' (575/6) out of which the new Jerusalem (*Rev.* 21/2–10) was thought to have come 575/12

end: (1)=object or purpose: 162/33–35 see titles of **Christ (4)**

(2)='saw to the end of fighting' 64/32 of figures, the Law 367/7–27

(3)=Ending: ultimate state, fulfilment: see **Christ (4)**

evil/Evil one: see also Devil:

is but one in all 59/30–31

and addiction 59/31–34

evil in people: 326/37 347/35–348/6 see also **measure** (A)

experiences of God: Fox readily recognised these in other Christians (123/3–33) but said that experiences were not enough in themselves; and that the greatest deceivers among the Jews and Christians had had great experiences 29/22–30/10

experimentally: 'this I knew experimentally', i.e. in personal experience, at first hand acquaintance, *experientially*; a vogue word in Fox's day; see also Changes in the Meaning of Words, p.28

Faith: the true **catholic** (qv) faith does not consist in formulated doctrines or beliefs (ie. creeds) but in a life of inner faithfulness, of inner obedience, that is, of trusting to, of having faith in the voice of God, like **Abraham** (qv); see also **law (2) of faith**:

see especially **social testimonies** (A) (a) (inner faithfulness) 16/35–17/8 28/19–23 56/34–57/5 281/37–282/5 318/12–19

(A) is the gift of God 29/1 318/12

is 'a mystery held in a pure conscience' (1 *Tim.* 3:9) 28/23

is precious and divine 318/13

is 'owned' by GF 529/6–7

is a secret belief 14/19–26

Christ is the author and finisher of it (*Heb.* 12:2) 17/1–2, 16–19 28/19–23 351/7–10

'What is not of faith is sin' (*Rom.* 14:23) 559/9–14

who are 'of faith' are 'of **Abraham**' (qv) (*Gal.* 3:7–29) 336/9–11

who are of faith are 'flesh of Christ's flesh and bone of his bone', i.e. part of his spiritual body (*Eph.* 5:30 *Gen.* 2:23) 336/10–11

(B) works by love and purifies the heart 529/8–9

gives victory 17/4 529/9–10

gives access to God (*Rom.* 5:2 *Eph.* 2:18 *Heb.* 10:19) 17/1–2 28/21–22 318/14–15 529/9–10 see **access to God**

(C) we should ask in the faith 15/21–22

we must be brought into and through it 16/35–17/1

'if you look out of the faith . . . you will be brought into bondage again' 17/3–5

we must abide in it 17/1–7:

'Mind the faith of Christ' 59/3–7

'Be faithful in your measures' 281/37–282/28

'By faith the mountains are subdued' 574/26–575/3

'None . . . come into the Faith of Jesus . . . but [unless] they come to feel it within' GM 133/36–37 3.230/20–23

Fall, the: Adam and Eve's second or alienated state (*Gen.* 3:1–24): Fox like his contemporaries took the Adam and Eve story literally and he appears serious in asking questions about life before and after the Fall (287/21–288/4). 'Before the Fall' represented mankind's state of innocence and happiness when they were obedient to God (665/17). Through obedience to God *again* by means of the power of God and Christ within, Fox held that men and women could be restored into Adam and Eve's state once more. His adoption of the term 'state' may mislead, since in his view mankind's spiritual condition is never static. Through disobedience the Fall can happen to every one individually at any time (see *ran out,* Fox's Vocabulary, p.26 above). Fox also uses this story like a modern teaching myth or parable in order to explain how we first became 'like gods knowing good and evil' (*Gen.* 3:5), or in other words, how mankind came to experience the work of the Light within (see **Light (2)**). In effect this de-historicises the story and gives it eternal validity.

see especially 367/28–368/38

'in the alienation from God' (*Eph.* 4:18) 36/38

man and woman separated from God 529/14–16

out of God's power 283/29–30

'the states of Adam' 121/27–122/10 166/22–167/6 283/22–30

'the sleepy heavy state', its death to be witnessed 33/21–28

fast (1): 'the true or Lord's fast':

implied in 727/5–18: Ellwood's fuller text, p.622 2.374/39: 'the true fast of the Lord is from debate and strife . . . that breaks the bands of wickedness and undoes every heavy burden, and breaks every yoke, and lets the oppressed go free, and deals bread to the hungry' (see *Isa.* 58:1–11)

fast (2): the false fast: 727/5–15

fasting, GF's periods of: 9/34 138/37 147/9

Father: God the Father: see also **God (2)**:

'the Father of Life drew me to his Son by his Spirit' 11/33

fear of God/the Lord, the: is 'the beginning of Wisdom, and knowledge of the holy is understanding' (*Prov.* 9:10); see also **knowledge of God; that of God (2)**:

see especially 193/20–195/4 (OC) *Doctr.* pp.163–169 4.208–215
p.xliv/13–22 (Penn); 'To fear God is to depart from sin and evil, . . .
such as depart not from sin and evil, fear not God' (4.210/1–4); 'The
hand of God is against those who do evil' (194/7–9); 'A quaking,
dread and fear come upon all who persecute those who are obedient'
(406/7–22); 'Stand up in the power of the Lord' (193/19–20) '. . . *that*
will make all nations to tremble and to quake' (194/15–16); 'Fear
and dread the Lord God . . . *then* his presence and wisdom and
counsel thou shalt have' (193/20–22); 'To them that fear thy Name
the secrets of thee are made manifest' (204/31–32); 'All Friends, let
the dread and majesty of God fill you' (386/5)
fellowship in/with Christ; see also Christ (2) (B); church (2);
Gospel(1) (A):
is in the holy Spirit 35/29
with the Son, the Father, the Scriptures and one another in the
Power and Spirit 199/25–29
figures: Fox's use of *figures* differs from its traditional use in 'types,
figures and shadows'. For the distinction see **types.** Fox also calls
them 'comparisons' or parables, although they are not in story form.
They are a simple kind of spiritual discipline which can be practised
anywhere by anyone who desires self-knowledge. By reflecting
upon the natures of *outward* **creation** (qv) — the things and people
of everyday life — and applying them to our own *inward* states by
allowing the Light to search us, Fox says, 'all may come to read
themselves, and see where they are'. This teaching is in the tradition
of *Isa.* 40:3–8 and *Lk.* 3:4,5,9. Examples are given below and under
nature (2). This spiritual teaching was the subject of one of Fox's
earliest papers (1654); the *Journal* written twenty years later contains numerous references to it; and it features regularly in his public
addresses. So we may reasonably infer that this form of spirituality
was practised by individuals when alone or in silent meetings. It was
addressed to every one, including 'you that are unlearned, outwardly, as to the letter, [and] cannot read the Scripture outwardly'.
see especially *Doctr.* pp.15–21 4.32–39 (1654); Gwyn pp.113–116;
nature (2): 'As mountains [are] without thee, so mountains [are]
within thee (see **mountains**) . . . As thou hearest the thunder
without thee, so thou mayest hear the thunder within thee, the voice

without, so the Voice within (477/26–33). These are figures . . . '
Although earlier similar forms of this spiritual teaching are known,
Fox has two folio pages at the beginning of the 1654 paper relating it
to his teaching about the Light of Christ in every one: 'As the Light
opens and exerciseth thy conscience, it will open (reveal the meaning of) the parables and figures . . . This Light of God, which gave
forth the Scripture, will, according to its measure, open the Scripture to you . . . The Lord [is] speaking low (probably ordinary,
everyday) things—comparisons like to that nature in man—[so] that
man may look upon the creation with that which is invisible (viz. the
Light), and there read himself. There thou mayest see wherever
thou goest' (from the 1654 paper).

figures (2): for the more restricted sense in which types are figures, see
types

Fire: the spiritual fire (God, a consuming fire *Heb.* 12:29; *Mt.* 3:11–
12):
God's pure, refiner's fire is within 14/31–32 419/28
'the spiritual fire tries (=tests) all things' (see 1 *Pet.* 1:7) 15/25
the Lord showed what can live 'in his holy refining fire' (*Mal.* 3:1–3)
15/25–28

flesh (1): 'flesh of Christ's flesh' (*Eph.* 5:30): (= of one mind and
spirit); see also **Abraham; church (2); faith** (A):
'. . . and bone of his bone' (cf. *Gen.* 2:23 29:14 etc.) 336/10–11

flesh (2), the; The world of the senses ('fleshly things'), the desires after
which are contrary to the **Law of the Spirit** (qv), e.g. 'devouring the
creation' (over-eating) 2/15–20; usually in figurative sense: ambi-
tion, envy, covetousness, pride, etc. 15/10–19; see also **earthly; lust;
will (2)**:
see especially 16/20–18/8 59/13–15
the flesh is 'contrary to', 'lusts against the Spirit' (*Gal.* 5:17) 17/33–
18/5
the world's knowledge is 'in the flesh' 10/34–11/5 309/35
the flesh will not give up to the will of God 14/36–15/3
apostates and 'fleshly knowledge' 10/34–11/5
the false minister 'sows to the flesh' (*Gal.* 6:8) 310/23–26
'the fleshly mind, spirit, will, live in disobedience' 16/20–23

fly (= to flee): fleeing 'in the winter' (*Mk* 13:18, *Mt.* 24:20): GF's spiritual interpretation of *Mk* 13, *Mt.* 24; the 'winter' is any time of tribulation and trial of faith, including persecution 283/36–284/7 429/24; 'flight' 283/42

Food: the spiritual food, Christ Jesus; see also **love (2)** and **(5)**; **meeting (1)**:
the **Life** of Christ (qv) is to be GF's spiritual food 19/29–20/3
a large crowd 'feeding upon' the spirit and power of Christ 279/22–25
the pre-condition of eating the spiritual food 38/28–33

forgiveness; see also Personality of Fox, p.12 above: GF forgives persecutors 93/30–34 94/3–9 99/1–34 254/18–25 386/23–26 xliv/29

forgiveness of God; see 'blot out'; mercies of God

Foundation: (= Christ, 1 *Cor.* 3:11); see **Christ(4)**: Friends were 'settled upon him, the Foundation' 371/24–28

Friends: Fox used this mode of address in letters to Friends and strangers, including opponents. He referred to Friends as a body by the same name, variously addressing them as 'Friends *in* the Lord' or '*in* the Lord Jesus Christ', or '*in* Christ Jesus'. Fox also writes (BJ 1.384/3) to 'Friends of the Lord', which connects directly with Jesus' words, 'You are my friends if you do whatever I command you' (*Jn* 15:14). Thus the earliest name adopted, '**Children** of the Light' (qv), and the one customarily used by Fox, 'the **people of God**' (qv), have in common with 'Friends' the idea of the disciples' obedience to God and Christ, which is the mark of members of the true Church. 'Society of Friends' dates from 1793 (BQ 570).
'All Friends everywhere who are friends of Christ . . . are friends of God through Christ Jesus' 8.25/12
(*Jn* 15:14 quoted) 'Here Christ called his disciples sometimes friends and sometimes brethren' (*Heb.* 2:11–12) 8.286/35–40

generation: the generation of Christ (*Isa.* 53:8): (those) begotten of the will of God 727/1–5

Ghost, Holy: Fox infrequently uses this archaic term (KJV) for the Holy Spirit except in quotations (32/27 35/29–31 40/17,21). He uses them interchangeably in 35/27–31 and 40/13–21. The interconnections are clear in 'This Comforter or Holy Ghost, whom Christ has sent, shall reprove the world of their sin, . . . So how are you reproved of your sin . . . if the Comforter be not come to you, according to Christ's promise? And, as the disciples of Christ then, so now, the Spirit of Truth, this Comforter, "leads into all Truth" (*Jn* 16:7–13)' *Doctr.* 419/11–31 5.89/11–42

glory: Fox's *Journal* throughout is marked by a sense of the glory of God:

O Lord of glory! 10/29 25/9–10

glory and Life shone over all 48/2 700/38

'the glory has been talked of, but now is possessed' 204/23–24

'Take care of (= have a care for) God's glory' 511/31 528/5

God (1): see also under the following topics:

access to God

Grace of God

image (=likeness) of God

Kingdom of God

knowledge of God

Law (5) of God (Old Testament)

Law (4) of God (in the heart)

Lord (3): Lord God

love (1) of God (God's love towards man)

love (2) of God (man's love towards God)

mercies of God

people of God

power (1)–(6)

presence of God

principle (2) of God

providence of God

Seed (2) (3) (4) of God (Christ the Word)

seed of God (other meanings)

Son of God (Christ, the Word)

sons of God ('by adoption') (*Rom.* 8:14,15 9:24–26)

Spirit of God

Teacher: the inward Teacher

'Theology'

that of God (1) and **(2)** in every man and woman

Voice of God and Christ

Wisdom of God

Witness of God

Word of God

Words of God
Work of God: see **God (2) (B)**
God (2)

(A)   is the Creator of all 661/5–37
is the Father of Life 11/33 175/19–21
is the Father of spirits (*Heb.* 12:9) 35/17
is a refining **fire** (qv) within us 14/32
is a God at hand 347/1 is coming 143/5
is to be worshipped 35/17–19
has the key to the door of Light and Life 11/32
has a glorious presence 455/1

(B)(+) blesses 'in the field and basket' (*Deut.* 28:3,5) 169/6–19
'brings down and sets up', 'kills and makes alive' (1 *Sam.*
2:6) 10/28
carries through dangers 661/5–37
commands us to hear the Son 666/1–4
(he alone) delivers 413/21
the Father of Life drew GF to his Son by his Spirit
11/33 213/3–4
dwells in people's hearts 8/8–19
fulfils his promise 12/37–13/4
gathers his people 143/6
loves us 13/32–33 16/23 19/24
'made all things' 25/23
made man 367/18–27
makes a 'fruitful field' of a wilderness 13/7–10 and makes a
wilderness 13/8
satisfies the hungry soul 13/2–6
(he alone) saves 413/21
sets justices to do justice 55/15
sets GF in prison for service to be done 67/28–33
shows us ourselves 12/3
speaks to man 11/18–27
speaks now by his Son's Spirit 666/7–9
spoke by his Son 666/7–8
'suffers' (= allows) injustice to be done 62/8–11
supports all who trust in him 413/21–22

teaches his people himself 112/32 143/5

teaches his people by his Spirit 74/6 114/32

teaches his ways 16/12–13

turns people to the Lord Jesus Christ by his Spirit 11/33 213/3–4

(C)   believe in him 60/25

'they were not to dispute of God and Christ, but to obey him' 51/22–23

'In the measure of the Life of God, wait for wisdom from God' 173/5–6 175/19–24

wait 'upon God for the redemption of the body' (*Rom.* 8:23) 15/10

wait for Wisdom, his presence and Power 79/3–29

'wait for the living food from the living God' 173/7–8

Gospel (1), the: is the power of God (*Rom.* 1:16): It is essential to grasp that Fox's use of *Gospel* is different from our current usage. His distinctive meaning was fundamental to his teaching and he maintained it with great consistency. He distinguishes between the Gospel as *the power of God* that saves all who believe (or, have faith, RSV) (*Rom.* 1:16) and the message *about* the Gospel—the 'glad tidings' or 'good news'—that 'the power of God is over all'. The power of God is everlasting (hence 'everlasting Gospel') and universal (*Rev.* 14:6). Thus we can meet *in* the Gospel and have fellowship *in* it. See also **authority; Bible (1); Gospel (2)** and **(3); government of Christ; power (3) of God:**

(A) is the power of God (*Rom.* 1:16) 83/1–9 115/19–21 176/12–14 445/26–35 520/14–21

is everlasting 202/22

is from heaven 339/29

is invisible 445/34–35

is pure 281/33–34 (*Rev.* 14:6)

is a living way that is revealed within GM 6/6–7 3.41/33–34

in it is the heavenly fellowship 339/24–35 and liberty 419/8

was preached before *Mt. Mk Lk.* and *Jn* were written or printed 445/26–30.

(B) brings 'Life and immortality to light' (2 *Tim.* 1:10) 16/30 83/1–3 155/16–17 281/33–36

Christ judges 'according to his invisible power', the Gospel 445/
32–35

(C) Waiting in the Light you will receive the power of God which is
the Gospel of Peace 176/12–13

Gospel (2): the gospel message; 'Though the outward declaration of the
gospel be taken sometimes for the gospel; yet it is but figuratively,
and by a metonymy [transferred sense]. For to speak properly, the
gospel is this inward power and life which preaches glad tidings in
the hearts of all men . . . and therefore it is said to be preached 'in
every creature under heaven': whereas there are many thousands of
men and women to whom the gospel [message] was never preached'
(Barclay, *Apology,* Prop.V.VI,§ 23) Examples of metonymy: 'the
bottle' for alcoholic drink *(Chamb.); '*the crown' for a
monarch *(Coll.):*

(A) is the Gospel of Christ 16/29
is the Gospel of Peace 176/13–14 *(Eph.* 6:15, *Rom.* 10:15)
is the Gospel of salvation 319/32
is to be preached to all nations 339/24–31

(B) the world is judged by it 445/33–34

Gospel (3): the gospel order: see also **Gospel; government; Grace of
God; Order (1); Wisdom (3) of God;** The order that arises in the
Church when the members live in the Gospel, the power of God,
under the government of the Spirit and Light of God and Christ:

(A) men's and women's meetings established in the order of the
Gospel 513/22, 27 520/17–23 525/21–23 527/1–2 623/12–17
monthly meetings: set up or settled in the order of the Gospel
513/26,27 514/36 525/21–23

(B) brings that which was driven away; cherishes the good and
reproves the evil 525/11–15

(C) 'keep the Gospel order and government of Christ Jesus' 631/
17–21 636/19–21

government: government of **Christ;** see also **Gospel order:**
'the increase of which has no end' *(Isa.* 9:6–7) 631/15–21 636/17–21
the **Grace of God** (qv) . . . the universal rule is to govern, rule, etc.
687/33–39

government (2): civil government; see also **power of God (9);
professions:**

source of civil power 386/5–15, 21–26 700/20–23

Grace of God (1 *Jn* 2:27, *Tit.* 2:11,12); see also **Anointing; Gospel order; salvation; Spirit of Truth; Teacher (1)** and **(2)**; see especially 34/10–27 272/22–37 687/30–39

(A) is your free Teacher 317/13–15

was and is 'the saints' Teacher' 335/20–23

is sufficient and saving 272/29 445/35–38

came by Jesus 12/38–13/1 34/10–12 272/24

'has appeared to all men' (*Tit.* 2:11,12) 34/20 272/29 496/34–497/20

'is the most fit, proper and universal rule . . . given to all mankind to rule, direct, govern and order their lives by' 687/37–39

is to be received 425/16

is to be obeyed 425/12 687/33–37

may be turned into wantonness 15/19–22

(B) brings salvation 34/13,20 530/1–10

establishes people's hearts (*Ps.* 112:8) 34/13–14 272/33

seasons people's words (*Col.* 4:6) 34/14–15 272/32

teaches to 'live godlily' . . . 'and deny ungodliness' 272/24–30 445/137–446/2 530/7–9

groans: the true and false groans (fig. = cries of distress) (cf. 'groan' *Jn* 11:33,38 *Rom.* 8:22,23,26) 14/34,37 15/7–12

ground (1): that in which something is rooted or supported, on which it stands, or from which it springs, grows or draws life:
  the ground of despair and temptations 5/35–36 6/14–16 of diseases 287/24

ground (2) (in people's hearts); see also **earth, hearts; seed (5)**:
  the fallow ground of the heart (*Jer.* 4:3) 39/30 122/5–7
  the Seed (= the Word (?)) of God lying thick in the ground or more probably 'the seed of God', the potential seed or people of God, waiting to be gathered 21/21–23
  plough up the fallow ground 263/17–21

growth: spiritual growth in the individual: see also **image; condition (3); measure; perfection; seed/Seed (1)**; Fox does not use the mustard seed as a metaphor of growth. Growing up in the Life of God he refers to as increasing one's **measure** (qv) of the Light and Life.

(A) is conditional upon obedience to the Anointing (= the Light) 59/3–7 340/39–341/3

is conditional upon our 'living in what we receive' 79/3–20

we grow up in Christ into perfection 688/1–36

people grow up in the image and power of the Almighty 28/2–5

(C) 'Wait in the Light, that you may grow up in the Life' *Journal* (1694) p.160

guidance: spiritual guidance; see also **Lord (1) (B); movings; Spirit of God (B); Teacher (2)**:

guidance and the power of God 592/15–593/4 593/12–14

Hand: the mighty hand of God (= the power of God, cf.**Arm**) 428/23

harvest: spiritual harvest in people's hearts 21/21–24

haste/hastiness/hasty (*Isa.* 28:16) 'Friends, be not hasty; for he who believes *in the Light* makes not haste' 175/14–15

hating the Light: 'he who does evil hates the Light' (*Jn* 3:20) see **Light (1) (C)**

healing: see Nickalls's index: cures, p.770; H. J. Cadbury's *GF's Book of Miracles* (CUP, 1648)

hearing: the true and false hearing: see especially 14/31–15/23

hearts: 'God dwells in people's hearts' 8/8–19 16/14–17 312/12–19. 'The Light shines in their hearts, and is not there the conscience?' GM p.13; see also **Blood (B); coming of Christ (3); conscience; Day of Christ (2) and (3); earth; Grace of God (B); Ground (2); Light (1) (A) and (B); ways (2); Word (2) of God (B) and (C)**

heaven (1): the heavenly man, the Speaker from heaven, see **Christ (4)**

heaven (2): a life beyond earthly existence 65/28–66/7 495/36–496/11 674/3–5

heaven (3): is within: see also **Jerusalem**

'[Thou sayest] thou never knew heaven in thyself, nor hell there, . . . [Yet] the Scriptures witness heaven within' 3.183/12,15

'Keep in the Power . . . that your lives and conversations (see Glossary) may be in heaven above the earth, [so] that they may preach to all [people] you have to deal with' 7.301/3–7

heaven (4): heaven signifies joy: [The voice from heaven] 'shakes the earth . . . [and] heaven also. The 'heaven' signifies joy, [and] so all the false joys . . . [in] any outward things . . . His voice shakes the earth and the heavens' 7.173/30–36

heirs: of Grace 272/22–36; of an endless life (*Heb.* 7:16) 311/35; and of Power 284/17–20

hell:

GF denies Christ was in hell three days and three nights 495/36–496/6

for 'such works lead people to hell' 578/1

cf. 'burning' 643/27–29; cf. 331/22–28 *the Word* burns, 'the unquenchable fire' (*Lk.* 3:16–17)

'hirelings' (*Jn* 10:12,13)(=paid ministers and clergy) 149/33–35: denounced by prophets and apostles 39/11–12

history of mankind: see also **apostasy; mankind; night of the apostasy; state (1) of Adam; teacher (4); types; war (2)**:

Adam (the state of Adam) 27/17–32 283/19–30 367/29–33 368/20–23

Adam to Moses 31/12–42 32/14–24, 30–40

Moses to the prophets and John the Baptist 31/19–27 32/14–19

Christ and the apostles 32/19–29

the **apostasy** (qv) 109/27–35

history: GF's knowledge of church history: see **Bible (2); intellect; martyrs**:

Foxe's 'Book of the Martyrs' (= *Acts and Monuments of the Christian Church, 1563)* 466/26–29 484/4–6 see also p.11 above

holiness: see **perfection**

honour (1): 'the honour of God', that comes from God only (*Jn* 5:44): that of God brings to seek the honour of God Ep. 53 7.68

Truth as an honour 341/8–11

honour (2): 'the world's honour (*Jn* 5:41–44) 36/27–37/9 86/21

hope: see also **Christ (4)**: a living hope rose in GF (1 *Pet.* 1:3 etc) 25/21–23

the Hope is Christ (*Col.* 1:27) 12/20–21 56/17–24 367/34–37

anchors the soul (*Heb.* 6:19) 14/22–23

humility: see **low** and cf. **haste.**

hungering after righteousness 12/37–13/6 see also **perfection**

image (= likeness) (*Gen.* 1:26) : 367/20; see also **growth**:

'renewed into the image of God by Christ Jesus' 27/22 367/18–27 368/24–29

people 'grow up in the image and power of the Almighty' 28/3–6

man and woman were in 'the image of God' 39/16,17

images: images made by man 36/8 367/18–19

imagination (1): false idea, whimsy 436/28–30

imagination(s) (2): In the 17th C. imagination had not acquired the modern sense, e.g. 'the creative imagination'. In the 1611 Bible it meant our thoughts, usually with evil or false connotations ('The imagination of man's heart is evil', *Gen.* 8:21 *Lk.* 1:51): 58/28 147/8

immediacy/immediate: i.e. with nothing between, with direct contact; not 'without delay':

the Lord's immediate Hand (= power) 329/21 428/23

his immediate Spirit and Power 34/25

infallibility: A subject of contemporary debate; if the Scriptures were dictated by the holy Spirit they were the infallible Word of God, but if the Spirit could be known apart from the Bible and in the same measure as in the apostles' time, as Fox argued, utterances made in the infallible Spirit are a possibility now: see also: **Bible (1)**:

this 'I infallibly knew' 35/6

fallibility of Popes 495/1–12

inner Light: No instance of this usage has been noted in Fox. It does not fit into his within/without and inward/outward categories. 'Inner' in 'inner/outer' merely indicates location and usually smaller size, as in 'Inner Circle'. 'Inward' indicates direction. 'Within' in Fox's usage refers to the world of mental and spiritual experience available when one turns the mind within: see also **inward**

inspiration: see **Bible (1)**

intellect: the inefficacy of 'wit or study or reading history in man's own will to declare or know the **generation** (qv) of Christ who was not begotten by the will of man but by the will of God' 727/1–5.

inventions: 'men's inventions' (= false ways of worship) (*Ps.* 106:29) 36/1–12 367/11–15

inward: see **inner Light**

inward Law (= the Light) 22/13–28

inward Light (rare usage) see **Light (1) (A)**

inward lust 22/13–28

inward man (2 *Cor.* 4:16) 46/36

inward parts (*Jer.* 31:33) 23/25–26

Israel: 'the house of spiritual Israel' (i.e. the true Christians (gentile and Jewish), the Jews in spirit, the obedient people of God):

'O let the house of spiritual Israel say, His mercy endures for ever' 13/6–7

'he [is] a Jew that is one inward' 114/29 see also **circumcision of the heart**

Fox 'brought people off from Jewish ceremonies' 36/1 see also **temple (1)**

Jacob, the star of Jacob (*Num.* 24:17,19) 29/35–36 see also **'Birth'**

Jerusalem: the new Jerusalem (*Gal.* 4:26 *Rev.* 21:2,10); see **heaven (2)** and **(3)**:

is above 530/118–531/17

who are within the Light of Christ and in his faith are members 575/5–31

is appeared 575/31

Jesus/Jesus Christ/Christ Jesus: To Fox, Jesus of Nazareth occupied a unique place in the history of the Jews as the promised prophet-Messiah (= Christ) (see **Prophet (1)**), as the 'Word made flesh' (see **Word (1)–(10)**), and as the **covenant** (qv) **of Light** (qv) to Jews and gentiles alike. Through the living Spirit of Christ we hear the voice of God or **words of God** (qv) addressed to us individually (cf.*Acts* 9:3–6) and as the **people** (qv) of God, teaching us the Way; see also **Christ (2); coming of the Christ; Light (1)** and **(4); Teacher (1), (2)** and **(4)**:

(A) Jesus is the Christ 203/11–204/26

on the cross 5/15–27

is the Way to the Father 13/19

is to have the pre-eminence 11/24–25

the Spirit and Light of Jesus 20/15

the unchangeable Truth is the Light of Jesus Christ 13/17–18

(B) Christ 'died for all' (*2 Cor.* 5:15), a propitiation for all (*1 Jn* 2:2) 34/16–19

'died for us', 'bought us' 154/4–7 see **cross (3)**

opens the Door of the Kingdom 13/35–36

(C) 'Wait in the Grace and Truth that comes by Jesus' 12/38–13/1

'So be meek and low; then you follow the example of Christ . . . whose back was struck, ... face spit upon, and yet cried, Father forgive them' Ep. 208 p.171/4–8 7.208/9–14

John the Baptist: see also **ministry (5)**:

his ministry 15/28–31
bore witness to the Light (*Jn* 1:7) 16/1–7
his ministry (31/15) is to be passed through 31/26–31 32/1–24
Joy (1) see also **cross (6)**; and 'rejoice' in **cross (5)** and **(9)**; 10/20 11/20
'my heart did leap for joy' 11/20
Joy (2): in the silent meeting 371/24–31
judgement (1): 'the saints shall judge the world' (1 *Cor.* 6:2,3) 135/7–9
184/23–24; see also **Day (3)**; **Providence**:
prophetic judgement 125/18–23
judgement (2): inward judgement see also **condemnations (3)**:
the Light judges 275/3–7
judged out of the book of conscience 143/30–31
judgement (3): God's 'judgement seat' (cf. *Jn* 19:13) 476/2–6
all to be brought 'before the judgement seat of Christ' (*Rom.* 14:10)
468/1–4
judgement (4) for disobedience 148/2–6 177/2–7 470/31–35 578/1 see
especially 194/1–32
judgements (5) on persecutors 493/18–23 504/16–505/14 566/25
justification: A subject of great controversy between Fox and his
contemporaries (see **perfection (1)**). He used 'just' for righteous;
'the Just One' for Jesus (*Acts* 3:13–15) and 'justification' for the
action by which men and women are made righteous (see **Christ (2)**
(B)). He defines the 'justified' thus: 'They that are in the Life are
justified; they are they who have unity with God and with one
another' (*The Papists' Strength, 1658* p.26). In accord with this view
Gwyn writes, 'Christ's work of *justifying* sinners cannot be separated from his *sanctifying* them by his inward guidance' (p.72).
Reference to **salvation** and **sanctification** is necessary.
'There is no justification out of the Light, out of Christ' 175/6–7
'Man cannot justify himself by the [outward] law . . . ; for he cannot
get out of that state but by abiding in the Light' 60/22–24
'There is no salvation, justification, sanctification, but to them who
believe in the Light' Ep. 265, p.297/40–41 8.9/42
Key: the heavenly key to the Kingdom (*Mt.*16:19) 13/33–36 see **King-
dom (1)** and **(2)**
Kingdom (1) of Christ: see also **Jesus (B)**; **Key**
Kingdom (2) of God:

is not of this world (*Jn* 18:36) 400/1–25 420/3–12

is set up 420/9–10

Kingdom (2) of God: see also **Jesus (B)**; **Key**; **Kingdom (1) of Christ; Light (1) (B)**:

The Kingdom has no geographical or denominational reference. Those who are 'ordered', 'ruled', 'governed', or 'reigned over' by God and Christ belong to the Kingdom in this life (31/30–31) and they can exclude themselves through disobedience (173/30–33) to the Law of God by not living in the Light:

see especially 173/30–40 175/6–8 400/1–24

'is everlasting' 15/30 31/30–31 34/37

'out of God's kingdom you are excluded' if you 'boast above your measure' 173/30–32

how 'all might come to be heirs' of it 152/20–25

its 'divine mysteries' opened 34/37

Knowledge of God and Christ (1):

'Knowledge of' in the Hebrew sense, meant knowledge gained through an intimate relationship, cf. 'Adam knew Eve' (*Gen.* 4:1). Knowledge of God and Christ comes only through obedience to the Law (cf. *Hos.* 4:1–3,6) of the Light, Spirit and Power (1 *Jn* 2:3–5); see also **Light (1) (B)**:

see especially 136/11–22

'none can know Christ by the Scriptures; none can know Christ but by revelation' 3.142/30–32

'no one upon the earth shall ever know Christ but by the Light' 3.197/36–37

'none knows the giver of this perfect Law [of God] but by the Spirit of God' 15/37

'in the Spirit and Grace of God and Light of Jesus . . . they might come to know Christ' 88/1–3 'and power' 103/29–32

in the Spirit 'we know that Christ did abide in us' (1 *Jn* 24) 51/35–36

knowledge (2), fleshly: see especially 17/21–23, 29–32 see also **Law (5)**: works death; is the apostates' knowledge 10/30–11/5

Lamb, the, (= Christ); see War, the Lamb's

Law (1) of Christ, the:

is the command of Christ 11/3

is to be fulfilled in his Power and Spirit 11/3

Law (2) of Faith, the: includes references to the **Law of Life, of Love,** and **of the Spirit:** see also **Faith;** the Jewish **Law (5):**
see especially 16/20–18/8
(A) is the Law of the Spirit 17/9
is the Law of Life 38/25–28
is the Law of Love 38/25–28
(B) frees from the law of sin and death 38/27–28
Law (3) of God, the; see also **Law (1), (2), (4), (7), (8), (9):**
see especially 15/32–16/1 22/13–23
(A) is in the mind 22/20–21
is pure and perfect 15/15–35
is known only by the Spirit of God 15/37 17/12–15
can be read and its Voice heard 15/38
was to be performed by the Jews, prophets and John 15/35–36
such as had 'the Life of the prophets and apostles . . . [and] Life of the Spirit of God' [were in] 'the Life of the Law' 4.84/3–11
(B) 'answers the perfect Principle of God in every one' 15/34
'answers that of God in every one' 29/2
'keep(s) the works of the flesh *under*' 15/33
'takes hold of the law of sin and death' 17/8–12
Law (4): the inward Law (*Mt.* 5:17–48): see **Law (3) of God:**
(A) 'the [inward] Law is the Light and the Light is the Life' 4.86/25
'the Life of the Law and the prophets is the Light' 4.77/1–2 4.78/29–30
(B) 'answers that of God in every one' 29/1–4
'brings one to love one's neighbour' 29/1–4
shows the inward lust 22/25–26
takes hold of the inward lust 22/27–28
Law (5): the (outward) Jewish Law; see also **justification:**
see especially 16/20–18/8
(A) was outward (*Mt.*5:17–48) 22/13–28 23/34–37 38/16–18 (OT)
is the law of sin and death 60/17–27
is a schoolmaster (*Gal.* 3:24) 16/28
is taken hold of by the Law of God 17/8–9
(B) was for the bringing in of the better Hope (Christ) 367/34–35
'took hold of the outward action' 22/27
made nothing perfect 367/34

judges and condemns 16/26–27

cannot justify 60/22–26 see also **justification**

(C) we are to become dead to it 16/36

we are freed from it by the Law of God 17/11–12

we are to be brought into and through it 16/35–36

law (6): the law of the land: see also **magistracy; civil authority:**

see especially 460/10–21 (1 *Pet.* 2:14) 559/4–34

and Christians 460/10–21

GF refuses legal redress for himself 254/23–25 see also **forgiveness**

the legal profession are out of the equity of God 28/33–29/6

Law (7): the law of Life: see **Law of Faith**

Law (8): the law of Love: see **Law of Faith**

Law (9): the law in the members: wars against the Law of God 22/20–22

Law (10): the outward law: see **Law (5)** and **(6)**

Law (11) 'the law of sin and death' (*Rom.* 8:2); see **Law (5) (A):**

17/8–12 38/28 60/17–23

Law (12) of the Spirit: see also **Law of Faith:**

see especially 15/32–18/8 17/8–11 38/25–28

(A) is the Love of God 16/23 17/9–10,16

comes by Jesus 17/10

(B) 'brings Life and immortality to light' 16/30

crosses the fleshly mind, spirit and will 16/20–17/15

frees us from the 'law of sin and death' (*Rom.* 8:2) 17/9–12

38/27–28

judges and condemns 16/27

Life: the Life in God (*Jn* 1:4); 'eternal', 'everlasting', 'endless', i.e.

timeless life, the world beyond time, 'the heavenly fellowship in the

Spirit' (154/4); see also **Light (1) (A)** and **(C); God (2) (A)** and **(C);**

knowledge of God; Principle (2); Son of God; sons of God; Word (3):

(A) is the knowledge of thee (the Lord) in the Spirit 10/30

is invisible 437/10

is solid 281/31

does not change 437/9

is to be lived in 340/14–15

suffers under the law of sin and death 60/19

(B) brings Scriptures to mind 13/28–31

guides up to the Father of Life 175/19–21

'rises' in Friends 43/11
'said it was done' 43/11
'struck at my Life' 39/3
'takes away the occasion of all wars' 65/10
(C) 'Feel his eternal life abiding in you; for 'he that has the Son of God has life' eternal (1 *Jn* 5:12) Ep. 184 7.172/32–33
'In the measure of Life wait' 175/19–20
'Do as it moves' 692/5–7
is to be lived in 62/12–15 cf. **deceivers**
Light (1), the: see also **Children of** (the Light); **Christ (2)** (A); con-demnation (1); conscience; Covenant (2); Day of Christ; grace of God; inner; inward; justification; Light (4)** and **Spirit; perfection (1); Principle (2); the Way (1):**
see especially 295/18–296/31 and **measure** 143/8–15
(A) 'Christ is the precious Light' GM 85/4–5 3.158/5
is divine 29/19 274/32 (OC) 303/2–22
is the gift of Christ 12/19–20
'is the Law [which] teaches you' 4.86/33 see also **Law (3)**
is the Light of Christ 122/12
is the Light in Christ and God 309/27 see **'Theology'**: God and Christ
is the Light of God 309/31–33
is the Light of Life (*Jn* 1:4 8:12) 33/9 274/33–34 295/31–34
is the Life in Christ the Word 319/20
is the Light of Jesus 35/8 88/2 236/33
is the Light of Jesus Christ 144/6 326/33–34
is but one 7.28 7.58
is spiritual, not natural 274/32 295/18–296/31
is the unchangeable Truth 13/17–18
is universal 'in every man' (*Jn* 1:9) 33/5–7 471/26–28 642/18–29 (Red Indian)
is the Way to God 35/4–5 283/15
is in all consciences 143/39
is 'in their own hearts' 115/15
is 'inward' (rare usage) 35/3
is over all 361/28
is in wicked men 471/18–25 496/32–497/18

is within 143/33 (Fox's normal usage)

is not the Scriptures 471/34–36

(B)(−) condemns all evil deeds 144/10 251/14–18

condemns the Devil 16/8

convinces (= convicts, condemns) 283/36–40

judges (*Jn* 3:20, 21) 275/3–7

lets people see their evil thoughts, words and actions 92/18–22 117/7–9

manifests all things 14/30 15/24

'reproves for sin' (*Jn* 3:20) 258/7–8

reveals what is out of the Light (darkness, etc.) 14/26–30

reveals the secrets of every one's heart 30/20–32 236/31–35

searches us thoroughly 31/8

shows the deceit of your hearts 135/26

shows we are strangers to the promise, without God, in darkness and death 117/14–17 (*Eph.* 2:12)

shows the (false) ways, religions, worships, teachers 304/19–21 305/20–21

shows our words and deeds 115/15–17

(+) brings 'to know Christ' 88/3 see **knowledge**

brings to know the virtues of the creatures 27/33–36

brings into unity 7.53

calls the mind within 309/27–28

'they that walk in this Light come to the mountain of God' (*Mic.* 4:1–4) 16/10–13

'comprehends time and the world' 175/39

enlightens every man (*Jn* 1:9) 16/4

fathoms the world 175/39

gathers people to God's teaching 27/14

'gave forth the Scriptures' 4.32/9

gives 'knowledge of the glory of God . . .' (2 *Cor.* 4:6) 295/23–25

guides to Christ from sin 48/20

'leads to the Kingdom of God' and gives entrance 173/34–37 see *Jn* 8:12

renews the minds 309/29

saves (*Isa.* 49:6) 296/24–27 see **salvation**

shows Christ always present 155/11–12

is sufficient to lead to Christ 318/8–11

teaches 34/24–27 see also the inward **Teacher; Grace of God**

teaches holiness and righteousness 143/22–27 144/12

teaches while we walk, lie down or work 115/18–19 144/12–13

teaches how to use the creatures 60/12

turns the mind to God 309/29 and to Christ 122/13

turns people to their salvation and way to God 35/4

(C)   abide in the Light 60/24

'become Children of the Light' 29/17 318/5–11 335/14–17 see **children of**

'believe in the Light' (*Jn* 12:36) 16/5–7 29/15 33/8–9 see *Jn* 12:36

come to the Light 92/18–25 237/10

dwell in the Light Ep. 54 p.53/39 7.69/19

feel the Light 205/6–7

take heed and hearken to the Light 309/26

'keep in the Light and Life' 175/24

love the Light 60/6–7 144/12 237/10

'mind the Light' 92/25–27 135/25

obey the Light 92/25–26

receive Christ '*in his Light*' 34/3–7

'stand still in the Light' see **still**

turn your minds in to the Light 309/25–26

wait 'to receive the power of God' 176/13 see also **wait**

'walk in the Light' (*Isa.* 2:5) 29/15–16 60/4–10

'in this Light you all walk in unity and sameness of mind' 4.17

they that are guided by it are one 7.18

hating the Light you hate Christ 135/27–28

disobeying the Light is your **condemnation** (qv) 135/27–28

Light (2): the teaching of the Light (negative and positive): Common experience shows that when seeking guidance we are often clearer about what not to do than about our right course of action. This reflects the fact that the Light operates negatively, by revealing 'that which is contrary in nature to itself', as well as positively. That the

Light acts negatively and positively is a constant feature of Fox's teaching (*Jn* 3:19–21): they see . . . their sins [−] *and* Christ [+] 89/14–16 117/10–19 225/33–36 he that shows sin [−] is he that takes it away [+] 64/12–13 see **Light (1) (B).** In contrast, Fox's use of **God, Christ** and **Jesus** is positive only (qv).

Light (3) and Power; see **state (1) of Adam**

Light (4) and Spirit, the: = **that of God in every one:** see also **that of God (1)** and **(2);** Fox constantly links 'Light' with 'Spirit' and in that sequence, thus maintaining the more specific experience of the Light in the conscience with the more general one of being moved by the Spirit:

Light and Spirit 33/15 35/3,7–8 335/37 642/21
Light and Spirit of Jesus 20/15 32/19–23
Light and Spirit of (Jesus) Christ 34/24–25 76/4 117/7–8
Light of Christ and Spirit of God 94/22 120/15–16
Light and Spirit of God 64/10 76/31–32 196/18

Light (5): see **inner; Light (1)(A)**

Lord (1): the Lord; see also **guidance; 'theology':**
see especially 58/26–59/2

(A) is/has come to teach his people himself (by his Spirit) 8/29–30 48/6 149/36
is the inward Teacher 8/28–30
is invisible 60/1–2

(B) 'bringest down and settest up' (1 *Sam.* 2:6) 10/28
commands to speak the Truth 51/11 124/23–24
commands GF to service 33/36
comforts by his Power 12/31–32
discovers all secret workings in man 58/26–27
fills with righteousness 13/1–7
fulfils his promise 13/1–2
gives sense and discerning of others' spirits 20/33–35
keeps (guards) us in greatest troubles 12/23–25
leads 11/34
lets GF see his love 11/34–35
'makes . . . a barren wilderness [into] a fruitful field' (*Isa.* 32:15) 10/26–27
moves (ministers) to speak 26/8–11 49/7

    moves to pray 49/12–13

    'opens' (people) 60/1 see Fox's Vocabulary p.26 above

    redeems 61/24

    reveals nature and virtue of the creatures 27/24–29

    sends GF into the world 34/3 see 'commands' immediately above

    (his Light) shines over all 370/5

    shows to man his thoughts 58/26

    speaks to GF 33/30–33

    teaches (see (A) above) 143/24–29

    upholds and preserves 428/26

(C) cast care upon the Lord 12/36–37

    keep the mind in to the Lord 30/18 58/26–35

    'All wait patiently upon the Lord' 12/37 58/27–33

    'O earth, hear the word of the Lord' (*Jer.* 22:29) 16/19–20

    ' . . . rely wholly upon the Lord alone' 10/11–16

Lord (2): the *power* of the Lord; see also **Arm; meeting (1)** see especially 44/1–16 (Name = power)

(A) is enjoyed in the silent meeting 449/23

    is over all 18/30 19/2

    is preached in 33/35–40

(B) breaks forth 21/28 42/17–19

    gains ground 23/38

    heals 44/1–3 45/14–18

    makes people tender 42/18–19

    moves GF to warn people 26/36–37

    opens (reveals) truth 20/2 see Fox's Vocabulary, p.26

    preserves 2/28 67/8

    shakes people 22/7 26/7

    shines 25/9–10

    refreshes 371/30

    upholds 67/8

    wrought (worked) upon people 41/10

Lord (3): the Lord God

  fulfils his promise 13/1–2

  moves (people) to speak 26/8–11

  satisfies the hungry soul 13/1–6

teaches 143/5

(and his Son) sent forth GF 34/38–35/1

Lord (4): the Lord Jesus: see especially 58/26–59/2

(A) the Spirit of the Lord Jesus is free 39/13–14

(B) discovers the roots of lusts and 'every principle' 58/33–59/2

(C) 'stand in the Faith of the Lord Jesus' 568/34

Lord (5): the Lord Jesus Christ: his Power is felt and received in the heart 202/33

Love (1): God's love towards mankind; see also **Law (12)**

see especially 277/5–14

(A) is dwelt in 228/15–16

is endless, eternal, everlasting 10/23 11/35

is experienced by GF 10/13–29 46/32–36

is great and infinite 13/32–33 14/10 19/21–28 ('an ocean') 21/6–9

is received 59/6–7

is tasted of 50/33

is unspeakable 35/32–38

(B) begets love 59/7

edifies (= builds up) 282/36

'makes a wilderness' and 'makes fruitful' 13/7–10

ravishes (transports, enraptures) 46/32–36 and strengthens 47/1–2 128/15–16

reveals man to himself 11/37–12/3

'takes up' GF 14/9

visits ('visitations of') 338/28

love (2): mankind's love for God;

(Friends') 439/4–6 507/27–32 623/35–624/2

bears the world's judgement 59/10–13

GF's (under persecution) 128/15–16

love (3) for the Fellowship 507/26–32

Love (4) Friends' love for GF 424/1–32 548/21–25 574/13–14 674/8–19

love (5) of one's neighbour 29/1–7 of enemies 380/5–7,16–24

love (6) of the world 473/21–32 all mankind 507/26–32

low: Fox taught the need to be humble and avoid spiritual pride (*Prov.* 11:2), as Jesus taught (*Mt.* 11:29). This constant feature is unconnected with the Nayler episode (1656) (as T. Edmund Harvey suggests in CJ p.xxvi) as it occurs at least as early as 1653. It is part of the discipline of 'waiting upon the Lord' (58/26–33) and not letting 'the mind go forth from God' (59/35–39 60/13–16 (1650))

'Keep low in your minds and learn of Christ who teaches you humility, to keep in it', EJ 478/3 2.232/33–34 347/6, 31

'Keep in the life of God to keep you low' 176/18–19

'Keep thy mind down low, up to the Lord God' 347/6

'And be low, waiting for the **coming** (qv) of the Lord Jesus in you all' (NPGF p.99)

lusts: inward lusts (e.g. 'worldly lusts' *Tit.* 2:12); lust for status, wealth, power, etc., not only sexual lust; see also **flesh (2):**
'the law of God shows the inward lust' 22/17–28
'the lusts of the flesh' 11/1–5 their root 58/35–59/2

magistracy: the 'magistrates sword' (1 *Pet.* 2:14 *Rom.* 13:4): see also **government; Law (6);** 197/34–35 400/37–401/3 460/10–21 699/16–700/13

man(kind): see also under **history of mankind:**
our unbelief 11/23–24
our state without God 11/20–27
our state in 'the earth' 13/10–19
how death passed upon all men 13/32–14/1

marriages: 421/20–422/22 519/16–37 see also **Gospel order; social testimonies**

martyrs: Fox was very much aware of his descent from martyr stock (1/17), and was familiar with Foxe's 'Book of Martyrs', (*Acts and Monuments of the Christian Church* 1563), which Queen Elizabeth caused to be placed in every parish church; see also **cross (7)–(10):** 72/31 (Lichfield) 214/11 (Essex) 351/2–5 453/4 461/3–5 466/26–29 484/4 (Book of) 676/31 680/22

measure: (used of spiritual gifts) given in limited but not fixed amount (see **growth**): e.g. 'the measure of faith' (*Rom.* 12:3); 'exalted above measure' (2 *Cor.* 12:7); 'the measure of the stature of the fulness of Christ' (*Eph.* 4:7,13,16): see especially 32/40 33/2 143/8–15 173/5–16 Ep. 16

(A) of the life of God 173/6
of the Spirit of God, 'according to your (capacity EJ)' 143/8–15
of the Spirit, Truth, Grace, Faith 331/8
of his Power and Life 281/36–37

is in evil people 143/8–14

(B) shows you sin etc. 143/10–14 see **faith** (C)

(C) 'mind your measure' 143/14

'in the measure of Life, wait' 175/19–20

'meat (= food) and drink' (fig. *Jn* 4:34 cf.*Mk* 10:38–39) 'My meat is to do the will of God' 193/27–31

meet help(s) (*Gen.* 2:18,20, 'an help meet for (Adam)'). Earlier form, help-meet; in 17 C., meet helps, i.e. men and women as helps meet (= fit, suitable) for one another, meet helps Ep. 320, p.370/4 (= helps-meet, Sharman, p.102/4–5); or with hyphen, Ep. 360 p. 434/31; but sometimes helps meet . . . e.g. Ep. 320, p.374/1

meeting (1): 'The silent meeting' (called so—not 'meeting for worship'—during Fox's lifetime) was wholly silent (283/1–2 359/33–35) or almost so from 1640's to 'about 1656' (282/7), when it changed in character (282/7–33 BQ pp.237, 237n, 372/3–7 (Swarthmoor). Fox approved speaking, praying and singing in the Spirit in 1657 (*Doctr.* pp.91–103 4.119–134) but the meeting with God was in the silence; see also **power of God (3)–(5); promise; sacraments; social testimonies** (B) **(3); wait; worship:**

'where two or three are gathered' 563/18–565/6

'the heavenly supper' (*Rev.* 3:20) 261/24–31

'Friends settled in the New Covenant' 441/16–17

meetings in silence 168/17–26 (FH) 314/23–33 340/30–36 446/11–27 449/8–24 cf.371/21–31 359/33–360/18

Experiences in the silent meeting:

the power of God preaches in the silence 283/1–6

the presence, power and spirit of God felt 359/33–35 360/12–15

the presence and power of the Lord felt 362/16–21 446/8–10 521/19–20

refreshings in the Lord (*Acts.* 3:19) 362/19–21 371/21–31 448/17–18

brokenness and Life flowed 545/10–13 blessed 442/30 fresh 647/3 glorious 647/3 heavenly 637/34 living 446/8 647/3 in peace 218/25 powerful 637/34 precious 445/11 thundering 637/34

meetings (2): other meetings; from the first, a second weekly meeting was held to care for physical needs of members, exhortation, discipline and fellowship. Meetings for other purposes were held later; see Nickalls's index 775; **gospel order; social testimonies (B) (3):**

functions 433/12 511/26–31 520/35–521/6

heats in meetings, due to over-crowding 427/3

mercies of God/Lord, etc.: The mercies of God are known when we are under judgement and hungering for the right way of life; 'the barren wilderness of our hearts' is made 'a fruitful field' (*Isa.* 32:15 1 *Sam.* 2:6); see also **blot out; forgiveness:**

see especially Ep. 10

Fox's experiences 10/20–31 12/23–25, 35–13/7 59/7–13

'endure for ever' (*Ps.* 106:1) 13/6–7

'in the greatest sorrows and temptations, . . . the Lord in his mercy kept me' 12/23–25

mind (1): see **faith** (C); **Light (1)** (B); **measure 433/12** (C); **virgin (2):** keep the mind in 30/17–19, mind him 58/35

mind (2) the fleshly mind (*Col.* 2:18) 59/13–15, 30–34; minds in bondage 13/11–17

mind (3) the running mind (= the mind that 'runs *out*') 147/23 i.e. that does not keep *in* to the Lord (30/18); see also **low;** *out* (out from) and *ran out* in Vocabulary p.26; 58/26–30

ministers and **ministry;** see also **perfection (1); reach; seed (5); sower; theological colleges; witness:**

ministers (1) of Christ: see especially 310/34–311/15

  (A) are in the Life in God 175/35

        are born of the Spirit, 310/27–28

        are in the eternal Spirit 17/24–25

        are 'sent by Christ' 235/9

        have Christ's Spirit 17/26, 27

        are not qualified by theological training 7/19–29 8/3

  (B) beget to God 175/36 437/6–7 (EB) see **beget**

        bring liberty and freedom 17/21

        divide (qv) the Word (cf. 2 *Tim.* 2:15) 125/22–23 271/1–2

        heal the mind and body 42/20–43/4 43/26–44/16 49/9–30

        minister to the Spirit of God in prison in every one 310/35–311/15

        must be *in* the Spirit 17/24–29

        preach freely 39/10–18 500/20–24

        sow to the Spirit 310/27–28

        'reach to that which is of God in every one' 341/5–6 see also

reach
reach to the Witness of God 179/20–21 302/2–5
reach people with God's Truth 438/3
turn people to the Spirit of God 273/6–11
use 'few and savoury words' 2/7
wait in patience 331/31–32
work to present every man perfect in Christ 688/22–27
ministry (2): man's ministry: see also **seedsmen (2)**: see especially 310/
13–31
(A) ministry of man and by man brings into bondage 17/20–23
can never bring any into Unity and Fellowship 17/28 36/1–14
(B) brings into bondage and under the shadow of death and darkness 17/23
ministry (3): the travelling ministry (Friends); the ministry of the
spoken word; see also **meeting (1); ministers (1) of Christ; women:**
see especially epistles to Friends in the public ministry on pp.174,
263, 340
they give forth from the Spirit 136/9–20
are moved by the power of God 327/37–328/18 329/19–22
speak out of the silence 360/1–7
wait for Power before speaking 294/5–11
GF's first woman convert to become a well-known travelling minister was Elizabeth Hooton: she was not his first convert, cf. 43n
ministry (4) of condemnation (2 *Cor.* 3:7,9); see **condemnation (2)**
ministry (5) of John the Baptist: 31/15–16, 27–29 32/1–13
John and 'the least in the Kingdom' 32/1–24
ministry (6) of the prophets: 31/23–31
ministry (7): the false ministry: 310/9–33
sows to the flesh 310/24–25
ministry (8): the paid ministry: 39/1–12 53/25–35 184/28–37 186/
8–188/9 (FD) 629/31–630/22 theological training of 7/19–29 8/2–5
36/4–7 310/20–21 333/15–334/19 (Durham)
ministry (9) of women: see also **social testimonies; women:** Elizabeth
Hooton: see **ministry (3)** above and Nickalls's index
Moses: see also **Adam to Moses: condemnation (2); Prophet;** 31/32–42
'the ministry of Moses' which restrains people from sin 31/12–42;
Moses' spirit 31/33

motion(s): see **movings**

mountains= mountains of sin and earthliness (*Lk.* 3:2–6) 32/8–9:
of sin and corruptions 113/31–32
of earth and 'imaginations' 336/1–2
are within 16/14–19 45/31–46/16
are brought down 31/28
are burned up 16/14

'mountain of the house of the Lord' (*Isa.* 2:2 *Mic.* 4:1–2) : 16/10–13

'movings' or 'motions': impulses of the Spirit, see also **guidance:**
to go to a place 24/2–6
to warn (reprove) oppressors and deceivers 26/32–27/9
to declare against 'Jewish ceremonies', 'vain traditions' etc. 36/
12–14
to go to a steeplehouse 26/9 and to gaols 355/28–34
to offer oneself (to suffer) 42/4

mystery: see under **faith**

naked (1): exposed to God's sight (*Heb.* 4:13): sins not 'covered'
(*Rom.* 4:7), not 'clothed with righteousness' (*Ps.* 132:9) 'Woe is to
every one that is covered, but not with the Spirit of the Lord' 7.35/
10–11

naked (2): unarmed, without arms or armour, see 255/34 255n3; fig.,
without 'the armour of God' (*Eph.* 6:13)
'All who hate the Light . . . are naked' *Doctr.* 848/25 'So the Light,
you see, is your Armour ['of Light'] (*Rom.* 13:12)' *Doctr.* 848/22,23
846/8 6.166/1–13

naked (3): partly or completely unclothed as a sign: see **signs;** Glossary

Name/name (1): In addition to the ordinary meaning (the name by
which someone or something is known) Fox uses 'name' in the
important Hebrew sense of the nature of a person, their character,
personality or spiritual being; thus one can be *in* or not *in* the Name
or Spirit of God; see also **Name (2)** and **(3); nature:**
people are gathered *into* it (125/37–126/2) or come *out* of it 122/1–10
'two or three meet *in* his Name' 564/25–26

Name (2) of God, Lord, etc.: Of the attributes of the Name (see **Name
(1)**) Fox in brief references usually chooses power: see **Power (1)–
(6):**
devils made subject *through* his Name 44/9–10

99

people gathered *into* his Name 125/37–38 241/8–9

name (3) of Jesus: see also **name/Name** above:

is above every other Name (*Phil.* 2:9,10) 125/38

'we are Christians and partake of the nature and life of Christ' (cf. 2*Pet.* 1:3,4) 559/30

no salvation *in* any other Name (*Acts* 4:12) 125/29–126/2

'gathered *into* the Name' (*Mt.* 18:20) 125/37 241/8 '*where* they have salvation and free teaching' 302/24–26

Name (4) of the Lord (i.e. the Power): is everlastingly over all 44/12–16

names: the many names: denominations: 'So look in whole Christendom and see what abundance of names there are . . . in the apostasy' 3.33/28–34

nature (1) (= the physical, material world): 'all things come by nature' (Vale of Beavor, now spelt Belvoir) 25/11–26

nature (2): First see **figures (1)**: Below are examples of Fox's 'figures'— simple 'parables' or 'comparisons' (368/6) used by him as a form of spiritual discipline. Meditating on the nature of things and people *without,* helps to reveal our spiritual condition *within:* 'The nature of things hurtful without are hurtful within, in the hearts and minds of wicked men' (19/13–16). 'People . . . do not see the nature of Cain, of Esau, of Judas in themselves . . . With the Light and Spirit of Truth to see into themselves, they came to cry, It is I, I, I, it is myself that has been the Ishmael, the Esau, etc.' (30/20–32). For the practice of this discipline Fox drew freely upon the whole of creation seen in the Bible: see especially 19/13–21 21/17–21 30/20–32 31/12–19 59/16–30 82/28–29 121/31–122/4 204/27–31 357/3–7 Ep. 390 (all)

1. Nature of Animals

wild asses (*Jer.* 2:24) = 'puffed up by pride', 'snuffing up' 121/37 205/18–26 'As asses without thee, snuffing up their noses upon the mountains, thou art lifted up in thy high-mindedness, and full of pride and wildness; thou wilt see thyself to be [like] a wild ass' *Doctr.* 17/46–49.

bulls of Bashan 'fat bulls of Bashan beset me round' (*Ps.* 22:12–13) 30/36 'as fat bulls without thee feeding the flesh, thou art a fat bull who feedest the flesh' *Doctr.* 17/32–33

dogs (*Jer.* 15:3) 'tear and devour' and 'bite the sheep' and one another 59/17–18 561/10–11

dragons: see *Isa.* 34:13 in vv.1–15 121/36

wild heifers (young cows): 'get the yoke on the wild heifer . . . ; save yourselves from a push, and bring them down' Ep. 195 p.152/45–50 7.186/31–33

horses: 'prance and vapour in their strength' 59/26–27 'see that you keep the bit in the wild horse's mouth . . . then with the Power he may be ordered; though he snuffs and snores, the bridle being kept in his mouth, he is held down by it' Ep. 195 p.152/45–50 7/186/33–38

lambs= Christians (*Jn* 21:15) 59/20 405/30

lions (*Ps.* 52:4 1 *Pet.* 5:8) 'tear, devour and destroy' 59/18–19

owls (*Isa.* 34:14) 121/36

serpents (*Ps.* 58:4) 'sting, envenom, and poison' 59/21–22

sheep= Christians (*Jn* 10:27) 405/28–30 561/10–13

swine 59/16 'wallowing in mire' 121/35 'biting and rending'

vipers (*Mt.* 3:7 'generation of vipers') 30/36

wolves (*Mt.* 7:6) people who 'tear, and devour Christians' 31/3 59/19–20

2. Nature of plants

see plant names 27/24–29

brambles 331/27

briery 33/34 331/27

cedars, tall (*Amos* 2:9 *Zech.* 11:1–2) 30/36; 'as tall cedars without thee, thou wilt see thyself a tall cedar, who livest without the truth, spreading thyself' *Doctr.* 17/40–41

chaffy 301/10

oaks (*Amos* 2:9 *Zech.* 11:2) 'sturdy oaks' 30/35 people 'who flourish and spread in [man's] wisdom and strength, who are strong in [doing much] evil, which must perish and come to the fire' 59/28–29 'thou in thy strength wilt see thyself as a strong oak, full of earth, and livest in power and dignity' *Doctr.* 17/42–43

thistles 121/35

thorny 33/34 (the world) 121/35 (human nature)

3. Things and places: see also **mountains; ways (2)**: 19/13–16

Babylon (= false religion) 21/18

Egypt (= state of slavery or bondage to sin) 19/18 21/17–19 29/28–29

Egyptian Sea (*Exod.* 14:27–28) 15/18–19 29/29 see **sea (2)**

grave, the 21/17–19 (the **earth** (qv) see 3/19–21 and *Ezek.* 37/1–14)
mountains 16/14–17
rough places 16/14–16
rubbish 18/14–17
Sodom 19/18 21/18
ways, crooked 16/14–17
wells without water (2 *Pet.* 2:17) 31/4
4. Biblical characters: see also **history of mankind:**
Abraham 'who are of faith are of Abraham' 336/8–10
Balaam (*Num.* 22:1 21 *Jude* 11) 'heard God's Voice' Ep. 390, 'could
speak the word of God' 29/33–37, erred from the Spirit of Christ 316/
34, loved 'the wages of unrighteousness' (*Jude* 11) 30/10–12
Cain (1 *Jn* 3:12): 'heard the voice of God' 29/28 19/17–19; was
warned and given a promise 316/31–32; was a persecutor 30/9, a
murdering spirit Ep. 390
Dathan (*Numbers* 16:1–35) (= gainsayer) 29/32 resisted Truth Ep.
390 *Ephraim* (*Hos.* 12:1): 'feeds upon wind . . . are like wild heifers'
(qv) 205/24–25
Esau see **'birth'**: his nature found within 74/18–20 (*Gen.* 25:29–34)
Ishmael (*Gen.* 17:20 21:9–21): his nature found within 19/17–19
74/18–20
Jacob: see **'Birth' (2)**
Judas: 'son of perdition' (*Jn* 17:12) betrayed Jesus outwardly: the
inward betrayal of Christ 46/11–13
Korah (=Core) (*Num.* 16: 1–36, *Jude* 11) resisted the Law 316/
33–34; Christians who resist the Gospel, or Truth; a gainsaying spirit
Ep. 390 p.501/28 8.246/17
Nimrod: The first powerful man, the 'mighty hunter before the
Lord' (*Gen.* 10:8–10), whose reputation suffered at the hands of
Fox, who apparently understood Nimrod not as having had the
honour of demonstrating his prowess before the Lord, but as hunt-
ing before the Lord hunted! Thus he became the archetypal figure
of those who speak or act before the Lord prompts them. Fox cites
those spirits 'that cannot be still, cannot be silent . . . , so cannot
keep at home [see p.27] in their houses, but are the hunters before
the Lord, like Nimrod the first builder of Babel' (*Gen.*
11:1–9) (*Doctr.* 103 4.134). The spiritual counsel is clear; perhaps we

may also learn the necessity for caution in the use of ambiguous prepositions.

Pharaoh (*Exod.* 5:1–2 7:14 etc.) 19/17–19

Saul (1 *Sam.* 18:8–9) of a persecuting nature 561/3–7

'night of the apostasy': see also **apostasy:**
see especially GM 66–67 3.132–133 339//21–24
Fox typically writes of 'the apostasy since the apostles' days' (100/20 3.132) and, rarely, 'the falling away from the Word of God was *before* the apostles' decease' (3.132/7 also), instancing the anti-Christs of 1 *Jn* 2:18,19 and 'all the world worshipping the dragon' (*Rev.* 13:2–8). 'The beginning of this state was a matter of 1600 years since' Ep. 239 p.217/33 7.262/34 (1662). Thus it began before the apostles died, becoming general 'a few ages after the apostles' (Ep. 287), but 'God hath never left himself without witnesses' (Ann. Cat. 5.128G).

notions: ideas 25/28 110/8; especially speculative, hypothetical ideas; 'airy notions' 19/37: notionist 75/9–10

obedience (*Deut.* 6:17); see also **deceivers; disobedience; Peace (1):**
see especially 401/22–23 665/16–17 (Paradise) 170/6–15
to Christ's commands (Scriptures) 245/30–32
to God and Christ 51/22–23
to God and man 170/6–15 466/23–469/29
to the Light 135/24–27
to the Lord 401/22–30 406/11
to the Truth of the Lord 400/26
God's requirings 401/22–25
'we resolve to hear the Son' 665/36–666/16

ocean of darkness and death 19/25 21/10 and Light and Love 19/26 see also **baptism (2)**

'offices of Christ' (= the work, service, roles or functions of Christ): A theological phrase current in 17th century to which GF gave a much fuller functional sense; see under **Christ (4), titles of; Christ (2) (B); Prophet:** 109/18–21 283/13–15 598/13–16 (Lyne)

open (1): to reveal (usual meaning): 6/7 12/14,18 27/28–29 34/22–31

open (2): to make a way into: 'opened me' 14/17–18

opening (3): revelation : 'what the Lord opened *in* me'; immediate openings 23/11–12 147/19

order (1)/ordering; see also under **Gospel Order; Grace of God; Wisdom of God** (the ordering principle):
see especially 173/7–29 175/19–27 194/28–33 364/35–36
'with the Wisdom of God you may be ordered . . . and with it . . . order all things under your hands' 322/3–7
'ordering fresh and green' 364/36
order (2): GF 'ordered' a school 520/8
parables: see also **figures (1); Seed (5); seedsmen (10):**
GF writes 'book' about parables, etc. 416/4: example 368/4–23
a part of GF's public preaching 109/25
the sower (*Mt.* 13) and Friends' principles 297/1–2 (TT)
the talents (*Mt.* 18:23–35 25:14–30) 624/9–15
the treasure in earthen vessels (2 *Cor.* 4:6–7) is the Light 296/30
the penny (*Mt.* 20:1–16) Ep. 16
Paradise of God: = heaven, heavenly state 665/16; is known in this Life: 27/17–28/6 ('the flaming sword'), 32/32 51/30 113/30(Moses) 496/3–10 665/16–31
parts, inward: 23/26
patience: see also **cross (9); ministry (1); sower; 'Word (5) of (my) patience'** (*Rev.* 2:2, 3 *Rev.* 3:10 *Jas.* 1:3–4 2 *Thess* 1:4):
patience in times of trial (*Rev.* 14:12) 283/36–284/11 311/26–29 386/12–15 405/12
'holy patience' 54/14–16
flesh cannot abide in the patience 14/36–15/28
sit *still* in the patience 284/1–10
Peace (1): inward peace (= peace with God, through the obedience of individual men and women): see also **access to God; Covenant (2); Gospel (2); temptations:** contrast the world's peace 12/30–35:
see especially 367/35–368/4
God's way is Peace 347/4
the first step to Peace 63/33 117/13 155/22–23 348/7
Peace in the power of God 48/12 193/35–40
'There is Peace in resting (see **rest**) in the Lord Jesus' 60/17–27
'Peace betwixt (men) and God' 235/10–19 281/16–18 303/22–28
part of GF's public preaching 155/22–23
Peace (2): the peace testimony: see under **social testimonies**
people of God, the; see also **church (2); covenant (2); elect; obedience:**

The fundamental OT and NT idea underlying GF's doctrine of the Church. True Christians are the people of God (2 *Cor.* 6:16 *Lev.* 26:11–12), the people of the New Covenant (*Jer.* 31:31) which superseded the Old Covenant (*Exod.* 19:5 *Deut.* 27:9,10), who are obedient to the Law in the heart, which is the Light; 104/4–19 (Pendle Hill) 106/31 (a group or Meeting) 143/5–6 277/25–29 709/10.

perfection (1) (*Mt.* 5:48 2 *Cor.* 13:11): GF believed that 'Be ye perfect' meant that men and women were in principle perfectible, to use modern terms. In other words, men and women are able through God's power to live in obedience to him and know 'righteousness, being renewed up into the state of Adam which he was in before he fell' (see **Fall, the**). Thus, perfection meant completed, grown up, mature, and not a permanent state of flawlessness (e.g. see *ran out*, Vocabulary p.27 above). Fox's opponents denied the *possibility* of 'perfection' (see note on 283/25 below); see also **justification; Law of God (3); ministers; patience; sanctification; sinless; state (1)** and **(2)**: see especially 18/27–30 56/6–57/7 61/15 134/2–10 166/23–167/6 367/28–368/33 688/1–689/3 (see 1 *Cor.* 10:13 'God is faithful etc.')

GF stands for purity, perfection, and righteousness 27/20–24 61/16

GF's opponents' views 18/27–30 56/14–15 57/3–5 166/22–167/6 216/20–27

GF's replies to his opponents 56/6–57/7 368/24–33

Adam's perfection; the origin of imperfection 166/23–167/6 367/28–368/33

the Church is to know Adam's state before he fell 283/21–28 (NB line 25: EJ reads 'cannot believe *a possibility* of coming') 27/22–24 32/30–40 283/21–28 367/21–368/23 688/28–31

Christ is able to restore man into 'that state that never fell, even to himself' (*Eph.* 4:13 'perfect man . . . the fulness of Christ') 27/29–32 368/24–33

the state in Christ 27/29–32 283/7–13 665/26–32

perfection in Christ 51/33–34 688/1–36

'perfection to the measure of the stature of the fulness of Christ' (*Eph.* 4:13) 32/30–33/4 135/11–19

the saints are to be perfected (*Mt.* 5:48 *Eph.* 4:12 2 *Cor.* 13:11) 135/15–16 'there is no perfection, but where there is sanctification' GM p.7/35 3.44/8

perfection comes through learning from Christ 216/20–27 665/ 26–666/16

perfection comes through faithfulness in the Power and Light 27/32–35

perfection and hope 56/17–25

'perfection (2) of troubles' (= deliverance under persecution) (cf. *Job*5:19): 277/10–14

places: see also **nature (3)**

rough places in people's hearts, made smooth 16/14–16

plants; see also **nature; growth:**

'the Lord's plants' (= Friends) 267/30 312/26–29

'plants of God' (= Friends) 168/29

pleading for sin: see **sin.**

plough: to 'plough up the fallow ground': the first stage of public ministry: to bring people to 'the Principle of God in them which they have transgressed' 122/5–7 263/17–19; the 'spiritual plough' ploughs up cloddy nature 331/28–29

portion: the Christian's lot or possession:

'The Gospel, the power of God, is the Christian's lot or possession' Ep. 61 7.74/20

'The Gospel, the power of God, . . . Know it to be your portion' 281/ 33–34

(suffering in innocency) 'knowing it to be your portion' in the world 404/31–37

possess; possession: contrasted with **profess,** etc. (qv); see **Christ (2) (A); glory:**

who *has* the Son of God *has* Life eternal 167/15–22

Truth, Christ, Glory, Son of God 'talked of but now is possessed' 204/21–26

Power (1) of Christ:

(A) is the eternal power of God 21/9–12, 15–17

is eternal and glorious 21/12

(B) brought GF through the ocean of death 21/10

enables GF to overcome temptation 21/9–12

speaks in man and woman 96/13–14
teaches 304/28–29

Power (2) of God and Christ: see also **'Theology'**: God and Christ
  (B) power of God brings into the power of Christ 21/19–21

Power (3) of God; see also **Christ (2)(A); cross (5); Gospel; Gospel order; Power (1)** and **(2):**
see especially 18/5–8 283/1–284/21
  (A) is the authority in meetings 514/6–14 520/14–21
      is the power of Christ within 21/9–17 (1 *Cor.* 1:24)
      is Christ within 96/18–19
      is the Cross 15/3 174/24–27 283/32 see **Cross (5)**
      is the **Crown** (qv)
      is everlasting 329/26
      is felt in meetings 28/8–12 179/22–27 Ep. 292 in the silence 283/1–2
      is felt in spiritual troubles 283/28–284/21 346/11–348/14
      is the Gospel (*Rom.* 1:16) 83/1–6 281/33–34 445/28
      is grown up in as we become subject to the Spirit of God 28/2–4
      is received 19/7 175/40–41 in the Light 176/13
      is 'set over the nation' 329/26
  (B) crucifies all that 'which is contrary to the will of God' 18/5–8 283/30–32
      preaches in the silence 283/1–6
      raised up many to praise God 19/7
      reaches the good in all 646/1
      speaks in man or woman 96/13–14
      'thundered among them' 51/23
      'wrought [worked] in a wonderful manner' 26/3–5
  (C) 'Be patient and still' (under spiritual trials) 283/36–284/21
      'Know the power of God in one another and in that rejoice' 174/24–26
      'Do as it moves' 692/5–7
      'Wait upon God to feel his Power' 79/3–13
      'The Gospel, the power of God, . . . Know it to be your **portion** (qv)' 281/33–34
      'Live every one in the Power of God' 284/17

Power (4) of God and the Lord; see also **Power of the Lord God:**

(A) is 'the authority in meetings' 514/6–14 520/14–21

(B) 'bound' people 179/19–21

gathered many 27/12–16

preserves, etc. 284/11–17

Power (5) of the Lord:

see especially 44/1–16 see also **professions**:

(A) was over all 18/30 19/2 361/27–28

can be abused 341/13–16

felt in a meeting 331/16–18 371/25–28

wonderfully manifested 26/1–3

Monthly Meetings settled in it 524/11

(B) breaks forth 21/28 27/12–16

carried GF over all opposition 36/22–23

chains all 372/7–8

gathered many 25/35–37 27/12–16

gives dominion (i.e. power over) 371/28

heals bodies and minds 44/1–3 128/17–21

moved many to declare everlasting Truth 26/8–11 331/11

moves to ministry 340/38–40

overturns the world 204/15–16

protects from arrest 442/4–5

raised up in court of law 389/14–22

'reached the witness of God in them' 179/19–20

seized upon MF (= caused to tremble) 116/28

settles disturbed minds 44/1

shines over all 361/27–28

'shook the nations' 21/15–17 and people 158/11–12

springs 19/3 389/17

stops from speaking 462/2–4

subdues all the contrary 175/41

wrought (worked) in wonderful manner 26/1–5

(C) 'Wait to feel the Lord's power' 79/14–15

keep in the power of the Lord 340/37–39

'Live in the Lord's power and life' 193/25

'Keep your meetings in the power of the Lord' 281/26

'Prize the power of the Lord and his Truth' 595/19

Power (6) of the Lord God: see especially 193/17–195/3 (OC) 263/1–16 moves GF 96/10–11

opens many mouths 26/7–8

'opened' (revealed) to GF 33/5–7

Power (7) and Light: see **state (1)**

Power (8) and Spirit 33/1–2 231/34 304/28–29 360/32 418/7–419/2 (in apostolic times)

Power (9): temporal (civil and political); government (2); magistracy: in political changes 386//5–15

Charles II reigns by the power of the Lord 386/21–22

religious freedom 559

Power (10): 'the dark power': 'the (OT) priests . . . acted by the dark power':29/22–23

Praise to God: GF praises God 13/2–6 44/12–16 661/5–37

Prayer: in the holy Spirit 22/29–23/2 35/27–33

'the house seemed to be shaken' 22/30–32

GF in prayer: xliv 13–22 (Penn)

an intercession is felt 583/32–36 584/2–5

prayings: the true and false prayings 14/31–15/23 (15/16); the world's 35/27–33

preaching: see also **heaven (3); ministry; power of God (3) (B); reach:** 'that your carriage and life may *preach*' (NB *not* 'speak') 263/30

presence of God; see GF's experiences throughout; **meeting (1); Christ (2) (A)**

'pride of life' (1 *Jn* 2:16); see whole paper 205/12–206/32: **lusts** (qv) of the eye and flesh 205/36–37

Priest/priest/priesthood (1): Christ as High Priest (*Heb*. 8 and 9); that died for them 155/9 see also **Christ (4)**

priest (2): 'the second priesthood' (1 *Pet*. 2:6–10) taught by Christ 237/1

priest (3): 'hireling priests' 39/1–18 69/2–12 (1*Cor*. 14:30,31): see also 2n

how they affect their flocks 624/9–15

the Levitical priesthood 500/16–24

principle (1): fundamental source from which something proceeds; the ultimate basis upon which the existence of something depends (OED)

Principle (2) of God: see also **answer:**

(A) 'the Principle of the Quakers is the Spirit of Christ' (*Rom.* 8:9) 699/16

the Principle of God 15/32–35 346/13,31–32 347/2–3,5,17,21–22 (Claypole)

of Life 90/6 of Light 90/6 of Truth (Justice Hotham) 90/6–15 118/23

is perfect in every one 15/34–35 see **perfection (1)**

is transgressed 347/3,16–18

(B) moulds up into patience, . . . stayedness 346/16–347/6

turns the mind to the Lord God 346/13–14

(C) come to the principle of God 347/5–6

'Be stayed in the principle of God in thee' 346/31–32

principle(s) (3): tenet(s) (and practice) of Friends and others 75/5 (Hotham) 495/24–35

'books of our principles' 213/24

Scriptural support 302/5–8

our principles peacable 439/12–13 (cf. 462/26)

tenets and particular testimonies 92/12–18 493/10–11 xxii/22

prince of darkness; see also **darkness; death; Devil; power** (10): 16/8–10 draws people from the Light 16/8–10

'prize your time': 55/32 91/13–14 92/22–23; see **time (2)**

profess/'professors'/profession: to profess Christ in words only (203/11); see also **possess; sin:**

contrasted with possess, possessors, possession of Christ 204/21–25 and the practice of Christianity 3/9–10 35/25–26 159/13–14 661/9

professors feed one another with words 19/34

professions: the three great professions—medical, clerical (clergy) and legal; see also **government; Wisdom of God:**

are out of the Wisdom of God 28/13–29/15

might be reformed by the power of the Lord 28/35–29/12

promise (1): the promise to the Seed (Christ) (*Gen.* 12:3 *Gal.* 3:8,16) 48/6–8

promise (2): to those who wait upon the Lord 12/37–13/2; see **Seed (1)– (4)**

'proof of Christ, the': (2 *Cor.* 13:3): the proof (of hearing Christ's voice) is in the Life and Light 176/3–4 (175/35–176/5)

prophecy (1): (=predictions and promises); cf. **types;** see also **promise;**

Prophet (1): 355/14–21 361/8–17

Deut. 18:18 Moses saw Christ the great Prophet 31/39–42 see **offices**

Dan. 2:1–45 the Kingdom that shall stand for ever 419/21–38

prophecy (2): (= receiving and giving a word from God); see **Word (7) of prophecy** (*Joel* 2: 28–9):

see especially 123/3–33 327/38–328/35 360/1–17

GF as a prophet 98/4 122/28–29 147/15–17 159/22–23

Friends moved to speak 26/8–11 26/36–27/3

Prophet (1): Jesus Christ as prophet (= teacher); see also **priesthood (2); prophecy (1):**

the Prophet that Moses spoke of (*Deut.* 18:18) 31/36–42 237/1–5 665/37

identified with Jesus (*Acts* 3:22 7:37); see **Christ (2) (B)**

prophet (2): see **ministry (6)** of the prophets; **prophecy (2)**

propitiation: (1 *Jn* 2:2 4:10 *Rom.* 3:25) 'It is clear that the word does not mean anything like the appeasing of an angry God, for the love of God is the starting-point (*Rom.* 3:24ff.). Professor C. H. Dodd assures us that the rendering "propitiation" is misleading, being in accord with the pagan usage but foreign to biblical usage'. D.M. Baillie, *God was in Christ,* p.187–8; see also *atonement* (Glossary); **cross (3); reconciliation:** 34/16–19 317/5 Ep. 355.

Providence; the providence of God: GF had a well-developed belief that monarchs and subjects alike are within God's providence, foresight and care. Friends had been 'preserved and supported . . . to be a peculiar, holy people to himself' . . . ' None can hurt a hair of your heads, except he suffer (= allow) it to try (= test) you' (BJ 2.503–504). Suffering through obedience (see **cross (6)–(11)** and **judgements** (qv) on persecutors) stands in apposition to Fox's confidence in God's protection during his travels in the ministry; see also **Day (3); judgements (4)** and **(5); will (1):**

see especially 386/5–15 424/15 576/7–30 661/5–662/18 (travels) 663/ 29–33

'orders all things to his glory' 612/15–25 664/9–12

the Lord 'sanctifies all things to me, the sea, etc.' 614/16–615/3 662/ 19–663/28 664/28–665/4

persecutions are suffered (= allowed) 386/14,15

pure (1) (*Mt.* 5:8) 'as a bell' 502/33–34 see **social testimonies**

pure (2) (*Mt.* 5:8) 'that which is pure in you'; see also **religion (1)**:
   (A) the pure Life of God in you 173/27
      'mind the pure Spirit of the everlasting God' 60/11
      'the Word of the Lord is pure' 1.368/26
   (B) guides to God Ep. 4
      joins us together Ep. 13
      may be lived and fed upon 7.64/15
   (C) 'Be kept in the pure Light up to God' 1/341/26
      'mind the pure Seed of God' Ep. 15
      'sink down in that which is pure' Ep. 10
      'stand still in it' Ep. 16
      'wait upon God in that which is pure' Ep. 16
purgatory: GF's disbelief in 529/6–16
'Quakers': (quake= to tremble) 200/23–35
   Justice Bennet 'first called us Quakers' (1650) 58/8
   are 'the Children of Light, called in scorn Quakers' 406/17–18 281/3
   are the elect people of God (*Col.* 3:12) 403/10; see **election; Israel**
   are not a sect 380/25–32
quiet(ness) (*Isa.* 30:15); see also **still(ness)**:
   'Be quiet and still' 43/55
   'in the Power . . . in the Light . . . be quiet' 283/40–41
ransom: see also **appeasement**: Used as a noun (1 *Tim.* 2:6 *Mt.* 20:28
   Mk 10:45) Ep. 355, or as a verb (*Jer.* 31:11) to rescue.
Ranters answered: 46/31–47/33
reach: minister to; see also **ministry (1)** and **(3)**:
   'reach to my **condition** (qv)' 6/26
   'reach that which is of God' 341/5–6
   people 'were reached with God's truth' (438/3) and Power 273/16–18
   and 'life and Light' 281/12–20:
   Captain Stoddart was reached 23/19
receive (*Jn* 1:12) : see **sons of God; Wisdom (3)** (A) and (C)
reconciliation: n. the establishing (or restoring) of fellowship between
   men and women and God ('peace with God')—in Fox's usage not
   only as a result of the sacrificial death of Jesus; see also **justification;
   Peace (1); propitiation; Word (8) of reconciliation** (2 *Cor.* 5:19):
   declared by GF 39/14 271/11–14
redeem: to 'buy back something that formerly belonged to the pur-

chaser' (F.J. Taylor): Christ's 'power and life and light' (redeems) 'from death to life, . . . from the power of Satan to God again' 283/13–18

Christ comes 'to redeem, **translate** (qv), **convert'**, see **condition (3)** 367/22 473/22

redemption: redemption of the body: see also **circumcision; conversion: creation:**

'redemption of the body' (*Rom.* 8:23) 15/9–10

'body of the sins of the flesh' (*Col.* 2:11) 38/28–33

'the outward body' and 'the body of death and sin' (*Deut.* 10:16 30:6) 166/34 167/6

regeneration: rebirth; see also **conversion:**

'from death to Life' 283/13–18

born again of the immortal Seed 531/9–10

rejoice : see **Joy (1)**

religion (1): pure religion (*Jas.* 1:27):

is to visit the fatherless, widows and strangers 35/22

is to keep from the spots of the world (2 *Pet.* 3:14) 35/23

all to come into it 339/24–31

religion (2): the world's religions; are vain 35/21 see **world (2)**

repentance; see also **condemnation (1)** of the Light:

preached by GF 25/13 34/2 90/33–36 121/11–19 144/5–18

and the restitution of goods 41/16–27

reprobation: state of being under the reproof or rebuke (= reprobation) of the Light; see also **election and reprobation:**

all who hate the Light are reprobated 317/10–12

Christ was in them except they be reprobates (2 *Cor.* 13:5) 96/12–13

Rest (= 'the Rest to the people of God' (*Heb.* 3:18–4:11)): the rest and peace in God which comes of trusting in the power of Christ, 'I therein saw clearly that all was done and to be done in and by Christ', and of abandoning one's own efforts of will to overcome evil (see Ep. 10): 'For as the apostle says, they that believe are entered into their Rest (*Heb.* 4:3) and have ceased from their works, as God did from his (*Heb.* 4:10). Now this Rest is an eternal rest in Christ (*Mt.* 11:28), the eternal Son of God . . . He is the eternal Rest, that gives eternal Life to his sheep'. EJ pp.527–8 (1694) 560/12–19

rest through abiding in the Light 60/22–27

resurrection (1) of Jesus Christ:
we own Christ Jesus, his coming, death and resurrection 559/6–7
references in NT 203/18–204/14
resurrection (2) (inward): for our resurrection see also **Birth (2); baptism (2); Paradise; Life:**
Christ, the Son of God, is come now 204/22–27
Christ is come . . . in the heart 261/26–34
the heavenly supper (*Rev.* 3:20) 261/30 see also **sacraments; silent meeting**
righteousness (1): upright living ('upright, that is, in righteousness' Ann. Cat. 8.199F) in accord with the inward Law of God; in other words, living in obedience to the Light within, which shows us what is unrighteous, and leads us to God and Christ, from whom we receive power to live uprightly. Since the Light reveals unjust dealings, this means that if we are faithful we live in justice with our fellows: see also **Law (3); Light (1)** (A): 'God is righteous, and he would have his people righteous, and to do righteously . . . God is just; and he would have his people to be just and do justly to all' (see whole passage EJ 571 BJ 2:457/32–458/3):
'Stand for God and his righteousness, in his Light and Life' 8.175/13:
'Everyone that has Christ has the righteousness of God wrought in him; and none own the righteousness of Christ but who own the Light that enlightens every man' 3.351/22–26
hungering after (*Deut.* 6:25 *Mt.* 5:6) 12/37–13/6
righteousness (2): GF a 'preacher of righteousness' 396/31
righteousness (3): the righteousness of Christ/God (*Rom.* 10:1–8); see **Christ (1)** (A)
existed before self-righteousness and man's righteousness 334/29–335/5
righteousness (4): of the Jewish Law ended (*Rom.* 10:5) 334/26–335/5
righteousness (5) of the world (*Jn* 16:8–11 *Rom.* 10:5) 472/5–18 '*their* righteousness and *their* judgement'; see **self-righteousness**
Roman Catholicism; see also **sacraments; traditions:** GF's attitude to; 495/1–496/11 538/1–32 676/12–13 690/21 692/35–39;
rubbish (in man's heart) burned up: 16/14
rudiments: 'beggarly rudiments' (cf. *Gal.* 4:9 *Col.* 2:20–23) 36/5, perhaps first principles; see also **elements (2); types**

rule: see **Grace of God**

'**sacraments, the**': the word is unscriptural 134/14; see also **baptism (2);
meeting (1); resurrection (2); supper:** The *Journal* deals very inade-
quately with GF's teaching about 'the two suppers' ('the last supper'
Lk. 22:14–20 and 'the heavenly supper' *Rev*. 3:20) and 'the two
baptisms', the baptism of John *Mt*. 3 and 'the baptism into one
Spirit' (see under **baptism (2)**). The principle reference is *Doctr*.
933–948 6.282–295

'The Lord's Supper':
GF's arguments against Roman Catholic doctrine 343/27–345/36

'The heavenly supper' (Rev. 3:20)
'doth sup with them and they with him' 261/26–31
'the Bread the saints break is . . . ' *(Jn* 6:25–58; 1 *Cor*. 10:16) 134/
11–19

sacrifice: the heavenly sacrifice, Christ Jesus: see also **cross (5)–(12):**
see especially 38/28–33
'the heavenly sacrifice, Christ Jesus, that true spiritual food'
38/30–31
'the great sacrifice, the Lord Jesus Christ, who offered himself for
the sin of the whole world' *(Heb.* 9:12,14) Ep. 216 7.218/18–20
'that one offering once for all' *(Heb.* 10:10) *Doctr*. 246/30–31 4.294/
8–9
'feeding upon the Bread of Life' (in the silent meeting) 449/22

saints: see also **perfection; sanctification:**
GF, 'whereof I am one' 135/8
'God dwells in them' (2 *Cor*. 6:16) 134/6
'the divinity dwells in them' *(Eph.* 4:6) 134/8
'they shall be made "partakers of the divine nature"' (2 *Pet*. 1:4)
134/9 559/30
'the saints shall judge the world' (1 *Cor*. 6:2–3) 135/7

salvation: It is necessary to look up all the cross-references given in this
entry. Fox held that Christ saves men and women *from* their sins and
not while still *in* their sins. This was an essential and distinctive
feature of his teaching; see also **Day (1); election; Grace of God;
justification; perfection (1); sanctification;**
'the Light . . . is saving, to them that believe in it' GM 184/36–37
3.306/28–29

is brought by the Grace of God 34/19–20 529/24–530/17

Christ in his Light (not 'Life' (Nickalls)) is saving 296/27 (*Isa.* 49:6)

Jesus Christ is God's salvation to the end of the earth 38/24 317/1–15

sanctification: the entries under **justification, perfection, saints, salvation,** with those below, outline Fox's teaching and indicate differences from contemporary doctrines. Compare the earlier state of John Burnyeat (1630–91); 'Though I lived in the act of sin, [I believed that] the guilt of it should not be charged upon me, but imputed to Christ, and his righteousness imputed to me. [But] I found it otherwise when I was turned to the Light, which did manifest all reproved things. Then I came to see the guilt remained' (*Journal* 1691) 51/19–31 134/28–34 368/24–29 GM p.284/1–8 3.450/3–12

'so far as a man is sanctified, *so far* he is justified and *no further;* for the same that sanctifies a man, justifies him' 3.450/5–12

'where Christ is within, there is sanctification, justification and redemption' GM p.158/33–34 3.267/36–37

'Justification and sanctification are one, for Christ, who is the Justification and Sanctification, is one' GM p.293/15–17 3.463/17–20

sanctuary: see **tabernacle: temple**

satan: see also **Devil:**

Satan tempts 4/14–19

the power of Satan 19/6 21/11 252/13

GF shown 'the depths of Satan' 34/35

saving: see **salvation**

Scriptures: see **Bible**

sea (1): the sea (= the world, *Jude* 13); see also **world (1)**: 'the world like a sea', since the apostles' days 30/12–13

'your faith will keep you to swim above them' (the waves and storms) 574/31–33

sea (2): fig. the Egyptian or Red Sea: its crossing represented escape from the bondage of false religion 29/29–30

sect(s): Quakers not a sect, but are in the power of God ('which was' (EJ)) before sects were (= existed) 380/25–27

Seed/seed (1): NB: Used with various meanings, of which the most important are as synonyms of Christ (see below), but not in connection with spiritual growth nor the growth or spread of the Kingdom of God; see also **growth; plants**

Seed (2): is Christ, the One (*Gal.* 3:16) *in whom* the promise to Abraham (*Gen.* 12:3 *Gal.* 3:8) that 'all nations shall be blessed' is fulfilled 48/8 178/29 339/16–23. The preposition *in* being important to Fox, the Seed is *in* all people, males and females, and they are *in* the Seed:

is Jesus Christ 336/18–21

is within 336/5–6 48/7–8 is felt within 336/19–21

is one in the male and female (*Gal.* 3:28) 74/23–24 184/19–21 339/19–20

the promise of God was to the Seed, Christ 233/22–23 348/9–11

Seed (3): Christ, the Seed of God, i.e. the Son of God:

  (A) the Seed of God in man 13/38

        the Seed of God that does not change 437/5

        the pure Seed of God Ep. 15

        'Friends in the noble Seed of God' 282/14

        the righteous Seed's sake 198/14

        the everlasting Seed of Life 276/18–19 288/22–23 368/37

        'his Seed is over all' 560/9–10 574/27 'reigns over all' 760/4

        'born again of incorruptible Seed' 24/11

  (C) 'Be . . . settled in the Seed of God' 437/5 (EB)

Seed (4): Christ, 'the seed of the woman' (*Gen.* 3:15) who 'bruises the Serpent's head', that is, overcomes sin and evil:

  (A) the Seed of the woman is Christ 337/36–338/19

  (B) 'bruised the head of the Serpent' 13/27–28 444/6–9 see also **Serpent**

  (C) 'in the Seed of Life dwell, which (who) bruises . . . ' 281/20–21

Seed (5): the ministry of the Word of God, parable of the sower (*Mk* 4:3 *Mt.* 13:18); see also **earth; ground (2); plough:**

in the fallow ground of the heart 122/5–7

'the Seed of God lying thick on the ground' 21/21–24 probably **Seed (8) of God**

'the Seed of God which (who) had long lain in death and bondage' 322/9–10 probably **seed (8) of God** (Nickalls has 'Seed')

'the Seed of God was raised out of the earth' 22/1–12

'bears seed [i.e. is fruitful] to God' 122/5–7

'brings forth heavenly and spiritual fruit' 331/24–32
(sing.) 'a seed of God in him (C. Fox)' 1/14

seed (6) of (= progeny, offspring, descendants (physical sense) (2 *Cor.*
11:22) seed of David according to the flesh 225/24–25

seed (7) of (= progeny, etc. of) Abraham (figurative sense): people of
faith: (*Gal.* 3:7) who are of faith are of Abraham 336/9–10

seed (8) of God: potential or actual Children of Light:
'the elect seed of God called Quakers' 281/3
'the Lord had a seed in those places' 302/23–24 (Cader Idris)
'his seed reached from sea to sea' 288/21 (Devon, Cornwall)
'I felt the seed of God to sparkle about me' 331/24–25 (Scotland)

seed (9) (progeny) of the Serpent = sins, temptations, etc. the Seed of
God (Christ) bruises (= overcomes, destroys) the seed of the Serpent 174/18

seeds(men) (10): the two seedsmen: those who sow (i.e. minister) to
the Spirit and those who sow to the flesh:
see especially 310/22–311/15
he who is made by the will of man reaps corruption 310/24–26
he who is born of the Spirit sows to the Spirit and reaps eternal Life
310/34–311/2

self-righteousness: (probably = self-willed, that is, living according to
one's own will, not God's, hence 'righteousness of man') 60/21 334/
29–335/7; see **righteousness (3)** and **(5)**

Serpent: see also **Devil; Seed (4); Teacher (3)** and **(4)**:
the second teacher in Paradise 665/17–18
the Destroyer 13/22–28
(speaks) in 'many people (who) *talked* of God and of Christ' 20/35–
21/1
the Serpent's head bruised 13/25–27

servant of the Lord (*Jn* 12:26) 307/12 cf. **sons of God (2)**

shadows: see **types**

sighing: the true and false sighing: true sighing is in the true Spirit
14/31–15/23

signs: Friends give warnings by 'signs' (*Isa.* 20:2–4): 407/27–408/26

silence: see **Christ (2) (B); meeting (1); words (2) of God**

sin = separation from God 529/15–16 see also **alienation; circumcision
of the heart; death:**

man is chained under darkness and sin 18/31

man 'concluded' (shut up) under sin (*Gal.* 3:22) 11/23

pleading for sin 18/27–30 56/7–8, 26–33 see also **professors**

sins of the flesh 38/30

sin against the holy Spirit 14/5

sins of mankind: Christ an offering for 5/24

singing; see also **meeting; worship:** Fox was opposed to formal singing. Reports of his own singing seem contradictory 6/1–2 (1645) 164/5–12 (1653) 377/8–9(1660):

'Friends broke out into singing' (*Eph.* 5:19) 541/30–33 (1669)

'sink down': see also **baptism (2):** An expression used by various early Friends. Probably adopted from Jacob Boehme. See Ep. 10 where 'Sink down in that which is pure' is equivalent to 'stand still in the Light' in the receiving of Power.

sinless: a 'holy and sinless life' 27/20–21: see **perfection**

smelling: To Fox's heightened spiritual sensitivities ('All things were new . . . All creation gave another smell unto me than before'), evil literally stank 43/7–8 537/22–26.

Social Testimonies and Witness (= Christian living, personal and corporate). These are dealt with in a special section on page 138.

Son of God (1): Jesus the Christ; see also the holy **thing:**

see especially 167/13–22 181/36–182/13 203/10–204/26 665/7–666/19

(A) is come 204/25–26

is one with the Father (*Jn* 10:30) 134/29–34

is set over all 167/12–22 182/14

is to be heard in all things 665/33

'This is my beloved Son' (*Mt.*17:5) 35/14

sent to be Saviour 35/33

Jesus was the Son of God 6/18–19

(B) gives eternal Life (*Jn* 10:10) 167/14–22

has given an understanding 204/25–26

sons of God (2) (*Jn* 1:12); Fox keeps a clear distinction between 'the sons of God' who 'receive' the power of the Word that was made flesh (*Jn* 1:12,14) and the more general or universal sense in which all people are 'children of God', by stressing that receiving the Power is dependent upon obedience to the Light (34/3–7). Some modern translations blur this distinction between 'children' and

'sons' which was important to Fox; see also **saints; sanctification:**
those who 'receive Christ *in his Light*' are given 'Power to become
sons of God, which I had obtained by receiving Christ' 34/3–7
who receive Christ have the Son of God and Life eternal 167/19
their relationship with the Father and the Son 134/29–34
sons of God and of the Day (of the Lord) 167/15–16
GF a 'son of God' 34/3–7 159/16–19 167/18 197/31 (*Jn* 1:12)

son of man (3): (*Dan*.7:13–14); rare usage: five instances in *Doctr.*
p.464 5.149–150

son of perdition (4); Judas: see also **nature (2)**
Judas (*Jn* 17:12) and the man of sin (2 *Thess.* 2:3) 46/6–14

soul: God has put into all men and women an immortal soul 8/38–9/4
417/11
the desires of the hungry soul satisfied 12/38–13/7

sound (1): v. to proclaim by word of mouth: abroad 640/29 641/10;
forth 202/22; out (1 *Thess.* 1:8) 467/38; through 301/4; (perhaps also)
amongst 299/6–8; with trumpets 356/24; speaking, speech 263/9

sound (2): adj.: wholesome, sound in spirit; n. 'a sound, precious
meeting' 643/13

sound (3): n. a narrow passage by water 625/17

sound (4): v. (naut.) to determine depth of sea-bottom 660/8–16

sound (5): v. (fig. naut. sense): as in 'to sound the Day of the Lord':
determining, by spiritually sensing, the location of separatist groups
of worshipping Christians: 78/20–22 and 79/3–29 (Cleveland); 104/
3–6 'a great people to be gathered' (Pendle Hill); 104/19–20 and 106/
29–34 (Sedbergh); 302/12–26 (probably Cader Idris)
(ministry through spoken words) 'sound deep to the Witness of
God' Ep.195

sower: see also **ministry (1)** and **(2); parables; seedsmen:**
the husbandman is patient 284/2–3 331/31–32

spark: divine spark: no instance of this expression noted cf. 283/5

sparkle: see **seed of God (8)**

Spirit of Christ (*Rom.* 8:9) 'the **principle** (qv) of the Quakers': see
especially 401/34–41 699/16–700/13
(A) Christ dwells in us by his Spirit 699/18
is not changeable 399/40–400/4
(B) brings us to seek peace and good of all men 699/25–26

guides 399/40

leads into all Truth 400/1–4 700/5–8

leads out of unrighteousness and ungodliness 699/19–20

moves people 400/2

is to be walked in 699/28–38

spirit of discerning: 122/28–29 155/29–35 159/22–23

spirit of evil: 542/17–543/1; see **Devil**

Spirit of God: Fox consistently associates Spirit with the Light, and therefore with Christ as the Light (see examples under **Light (4)** and **Spirit**) in contradistinction to charismatic theologies where the Spirit appears to be central and obedience to the Light under-stressed; see **Bible (1); Ghost, Holy; Law (3); Law (12) of the Spirit; Light (4) and Spirit; ministry (1)** and **(3); Power(8) and Spirit; pure (2); singing; Spirit, Holy; Sword (1) of the Spirit; 'Theology':**

see especially 15/16–16/1 16/20–18/8 28/2–6 32/40–33/20 34/3–27 34/38–35/9 103/24–34 ('10 miles about [= around]') 136/9–22

(A) is given to every man to profit with 34/21

is hated, rebelled against, resisted (*Acts* 7:51) 15/19–24

is immediate 34/25

is in wicked people 472/19–22

is infallible 495/10–12

is invisible 15/12

is that by which Power is received 181/20–23

is the touchstone and judge of doctrines 40/1–21

is universal 471/13–28

is 'vexed' (*Isa.* 63:10), 'quenched' (1 *Thess.* 5:19), 'grieved' (*Eph.* 4:30) 471/21–25

(B) brings into Joy, Peace, and Life 60/13–14

brings people off from their own ways 35/8

brings people to wait upon the Lord 58/31–32

enables one to discern the false 15/12–15

exalts 'valleys' in man 32/9

gave forth the Scriptures 33/16–20

'groans' (*Rom.* 8:26) 15/7–8

judges the evil 60/13

lays low mountains of sin and earthliness 32/8–9

leads into all Truth 34/9 271/6 of the Scriptures 235/17

leads to God 51/13 Christ and God 136/12–15 217/34–35

lusts against the flesh (*Gal.* 5:17) 17/36

makes crooked nature straight 32/4–5

makes hypocrites 'bring forth fruits for repentance' 32/7–8

makes intercession (*Rom.* 8:26) 15/8

makes rough nature smooth 32/5

mortifies (= kills) that which wars against it 17/35 460/11–16

never deceives any 35/5–6

opens the Scriptures 235/17 271/6 see **open (1)**

opens us 15/7–8 see **open (2)**

prepares a way for the Lord in man 32/10

shows you sin, etc., all the works of darkness 143/10–14

shows how to use the creatures 60/12

teaches 51/12 60/12

teaches to know how death reigned from Adam to Moses, etc., 31/12–31 32/12–19 see also **history of mankind**

teaches to know God 15/37

teaches to hear the Voice of the Law of God 15/38

turns people's minds to God, and to Christ and God their Teacher 79/14–17 136/12–15 217/34–35 to the Lord 360/31–32 to the Lord Jesus Christ 213/3–5 360/31–32

(C) all must come to that Spirit that gave forth the Scriptures 33/15–20

all must 'come into subjection to the Spirit' 28/3

all to come to the Spirit of God in themselves if they would know God, Christ, etc. 33/17–18 136/11–22 155/3–5

the fruits of the Spirit are love, righteousness, goodness, temperance etc. (*Gal.* 5:22–23 *Eph.* 5:9) 699/35–36

all 'to have heavenly fellowship in the Spirit' 155/5

is to be known as in the apostles' times 419/29

let not the mind go forth from the Spirit of God 60/13–16

'to live and walk in the Spirit of God is Joy, Peace and Life' 60/13–14

'mind the pure Spirit of the everlasting God' 60/11–16

'mind your measure of the Spirit of God' 143/11

'Quench not the Spirit' (1 *Thess.* 5:19): 18/1–4 Ep.69 Ep.355

Spirit, holy: see **Ghost, holy**

Spirit of the Lord:
    'Submit to the Spirit of the Lord' 58/31–32
Spirit of Truth (*Jn* 16:13); see also **Ghost, Holy; Grace of God; Spirit of God; Truth:**
    (A) 'is in the inward parts' 35/16
        is to be worshipped in 35/18
        was sent to the disciples 335/18–19
    (B) leads into all truth 34/9 235/15–19 472/7–10
        leads into the truth of the prophets, Christ's and apostles' words 109/39–41
        'reproves the world of sin, of righteousness, etc.' (*Jn* 16:8–11 472/8–10
Star/stars:
    (1): the bright and morning Star (*Rev.* 22:16); **Day-star** (2 *Pet.* 1:19) see **Christ (4)**
    (2): celestial bodies: 25/18
    (3) 'the wandering stars' (*Jude* 13), = false teachers (*Jude* 4), are without (cf. **Star (1)**) 122/3
star-gazers: 'drew people's minds from Christ, the bright and morning star' 38/34
state (1): the state of Adam before he fell; see also the **Fall; history of mankind:**
    all must come to know Adam's first state 31/20–23 283/7–35
    'such as were faithful . . . in the Power and Light of Christ should come into that state' 27/32–38
    'I was . . . come up into that state in which Adam was before he fell, in which the admirable works of the creation, and the virtues thereof, may be known' 27/22–32
state (2): man's state in Christ Jesus:
    Fox 'sees into another and more steadfast state than Adam's in innocency, even into a state in Christ Jesus, that should never fall' 27/30–32
state (3): inward states or 'conditions' 5/37 12/33,38 19/19–24 58/31
    the Scriptures to be applied to our own states 31/12–19
stature of Christ, of the fulness of the, (*Eph.* 4:13): 32/30–42
steeplehouse: a Puritan name for a parish church:
    is 'an old house made up of lime, stones and wood' 24/17–26

is not 'the Church' 500/4–15
is idolised by people 85/25–37
is not to be desecrated with bloodshed 99/32–34
are not 'dreadful houses of God' 109/8 168/4–9
GF spoke in steeplehouses to gather people thence 85/25–27
still(ness): see also **meeting (1); patience; Peace (1); quiet:**
'be still' (OC) (*Ps.* 46:10) 193/17 346–348 (Claypole letter) 692/6–7
sit still (*Isa.* 30:7) 284/1 340/31–35
stand still (2 *Chr.* 20:17) in the Light (= 'the first step to Peace')
117/13 176/11 284/8 and Power 283/40–284/15 and Life 692/6 and see
salvation 284/8 561/13–14 cf.58/31–38 Ep. 10
'stumble at' : to meet a serious difficulty to belief (1 *Pet.* 2:6–8, cf.
*Jn*11:9):
they that hate the Light, stumble at it 175/32–34
subjection to the will of God: 28/2–5 see **growth**
Substance: see **Christ (4)**
suffering: (*Phil.*1:29) : 400/26–401/41 Ep.398. see also **cross (5)–(12)**
summer, the: the time following a period of spiritual difficulty (*Mt.*
24:20, *Mk* 13:18) 283/36–284/11 cf. **winter**
supper (1) the heavenly supper (*Rev.* 3:20): 261/27–30: see also **silent
meeting; sacraments**
Supper (2): the Lord's supper: see **Sacraments**
Sword (1) of the Spirit (= the Word of God, *Eph.* 6:17); see also **Spirit
of God:**
cuts down corruptions 306/28–29
cuts down sin and evil 699/31
sword (2): 'the flaming sword' (*Gen.* 3:24) 27/17–18
sword (3): the outward sword, outward weapon = physical weapons:
399/12 402/15–16
tabernacle (1): a movable tent constructed as a sanctuary wherein God
might dwell among the Hebrews on their journeys (*Exod.* 25:8, 9 in
Exod. 25–27)
tabernacle (2): the human body (2 *Cor.* 5:1 2 *Pet.* 1:13); the Lord's
tabernacle:
the Lord comes into it 16/16 312/9–10
is 'to be found in man's heart' 16/14–17 312/9–10
Teacher (1): the teacher of righteousness or Prophet: the inward, true

Teacher: Fox's affirmation that 'God and Christ has come to teach his people himself' (98/13 105/4) is an essential distinctive feature of his teaching; see also **Anointing; Christ (2)** (A); **Grace of God;** the **Light (1)** (B); **Lord (1)** (A) and (B); **Teacher (4); 'Theology'; God and Christ:**

(A) is the Anointing (1 *Jn* 2:27) 8/29 20/4–17 59/3–7

is Christ 'that died for them' 190/35

is Christ their (free Teacher) 120/18 190/35 214/9 271/16–20

is God and Christ 98/13 105/4 120/17–18 152/18–28 see **'Theology'**

is the Lord Jesus Christ/Christ Jesus 95/22 157/34 168/24 213/4–16

is 'the Grace of God' 335/20–23 445/35–38 448/14–16

is the Spirit and Light of Jesus 20/15 cf. 196/13–20 74/5,6

is the heavenly Prophet 237/1–5

is (the Lord) God, Christ and the Spirit 74/5,6 149/36 152/18–28

the Lord (God) teaches his people 8/30 80/5 143/1–6

God speaks to them now by his Son 666/1–16

is the people's own Teacher 624/9–15

is 'the true Teacher' 80/3 107/12 149/33–34

is everywhere available to us 155/19–20 (*Ps.* 4:4)

is within 143/1–7, 33–35

Teacher (2); the inward Teacher—negative and positive guidance: 117/13–19 303/13–17 304/1–2 305/19–23 see also under **Light (2)**

teacher (3): the false teacher (the **Serpent**):

head of all false teachers 665/23–25

teacher (4): the three teachers: the first teacher was God, in Paradise 665/16; the second teacher was the Serpent 665/18; the third teacher was Christ Jesus 665/21–22

teaching (1) the apostles' free teaching 294/27

teaching (2); man's false teaching:

people to 'come off from all men's teaching' 50/4–5

false teachers ('hirelings' *Jn* 10:12–13) 76/2–3 186/12–187/36

temple (1): the Jew's temple (1 *Kn.* 6 2 *Chr.* 3):

God commanded it to be built (for a time) 8/17–18 125/33 351/24 was ended by Christ's coming 125/29–34

Temple (2): the spiritual temple (*Acts* 7:48 (Stephen), 1 *Cor.* 3:16 etc.

cf. 2 *Chron.* 2:6); see also **Church**
God does not 'dwell in temples made with hands' 8/8–19 20/16
is in people's hearts 8/14–17
his people are God's temple (8/19) and God dwells in them (2 *Cor.*
6:16 85/32–35 125/34–126/19

temptations: see also inward **Peace (1);** the **Seed (4)** of the woman;
troubles: Fox's Christian message is for all who need healing of
spirit, mind and body. Freedom from addictions and from idolising
the things of this world was a constant theme of his. Counsel to those
under great temptation or in **despair** (qv) occurs early and late in his
writings:
appear in the Light 14/26–30
are trials of faith 14/15–17
'Whatever you are addicted to the Tempter will come in that thing'
Ep. 10 59/30–34
GF's temptation: 'all things come by nature' 25/15–26 (Beavor=
Belvoir)
GF seeks the ground of temptations and despair 4/4–23 5/36 6/14
12/19–25
overcoming temptations 283/36–284/21 346/7–348/14 (Lady
Claypole)
are overcome by Christ 12/13–17
sin against the holy Spirit 21/31–38

Tempter, the: 21/31 see also **Devil**

tender= sensitive (usually); sometimes, sympathetic: the tender Thing
in man 18/32 (see **Thing**)
tender people 10/12 (young man) 23/22–24
tender conscience 456/28 467/17–29 482/22–23

testimonies: see **social testimonies**

'that of God (1) in every one' (cf. *Jn* 1:9 'the true Light lights every man'
188/7): According to T. Canby Jones 'in every one' is the commonest
form in the *Epistles.* But 'in every man and woman', 'in all', and 'in
all people' also occur; see also **Light (4); pure (2):**
29/1–4 253/5,32 281/10

that of God (2): in their consciences: see also **conscience:** 'that of God in
their consciences' (the Light of Christ Jesus in them) 188/10–11
206/13 483/1–2 175/27 guides

that which is pure: see **pure**

theological colleges: 333/15–334/19 (Durham):

a knowledge of languages is not saving 458/13–26

theological training does not qualify men to be ministers of Christ (Oxford and Cambridge) 7/18–29 8/2–7 11/6–8

'Theology': Out of many theological ideas classified in this Concordance, I have separated out under this heading, purely for reasons of convenience, some typical examples of Fox's use of variants of biblical names of God the Father, Jesus the Christ and the Spirit of God. See also **son of man.** They illustrate how Fox understood their relationships, but need to be supplemented by references in the main index: **God; Word (2),** etc. For the elucidation of Fox's teaching about the inward Christ and the historical Jesus, the Nickalls edition is of limited use as a sole source (see God and Christ below). Other works should be consulted: *Epistles, Doctrinals, The Great Mystery* (GM): e.g. *Atonement,* 'None know the atonement of Christ but by the Light within' GM 3.121

see especially 699/16—700/29

God 8/8–9 Creator 664/29–33 over all

God almighty 143/31

God the Father 24/27–28

God (= Lord) Lord (= God) 8/8–25 59/35–60/2 336/18–19

Lord God 664/28–33

God and Christ: Constructions such as 'God and Christ was come to teach his people himself' are very typical of Fox. But they were unacceptable to Ellwood (1694) for theological or grammatical reasons and from such sentences he omits either 'God' or 'Christ', or re-phrases the sentence or omits it altogether. In many cases the Nickalls edition restores the original wording, but not in all, e.g. 104/13 insert 'God and'; 111/36 alter to 'Christ and God's'. For a thorough study of this particular point the original text of the Cambridge Journal (1911) should be used.

Examples of 'God and Christ' followed by singular words: 'him' 11/29–32 51/22 54/24–25; 'his' 103/28; 'teaches' 98/13 120/18 152/24; 'Voice of' 123/23 152/26; 'their Saviour' 303/32, For Fox, in such contexts, God and Christ refer to the same entity. Thus he says 'Hearing the Son, we hear the Father also': see also **Light (1) (A);**

Son of God; Truth (A); **Word (2)**
Jesus/Jesus Christ/Christ Jesus: see main entries; the Lord Christ Jesus 34/24–25 58/34 107/8–9 and the Light 326/36
Christ the Word see **Word (2)**
the Lord, God and his son 34/38–35/2 666/1–16 sent GF forth
the Lord the Creator and his Son Jesus Christ 12/28–29
the Lord and (his) Christ 96/22–23 152/24 400/18
Father and Son 665/22–23 'my beloved Son'; 666/1–4 'hearing the Son we hear the Father also' (*Heb.* 1:1–2) 203/10–29
see **Spirit of God; Ghost, holy**
God, Christ, and the/his Spirit 34/24–25 666/7–9 'speaks now by his Spirit' (*Heb.* 1:1–2)
God/Father, Christ/Son with holy Spirit 125/35–36 217/34–36 666/7–9
drew GF to his Son by his Spirit 11/33
God and the Devil 212/26–36 see also **Devil; evil:**
Thing= the Son of God (cf. *Luke* 1:35) or Spirit of God 340/10–13 341/24
'quenched the tender Thing in them' (see 1 *Thess.*5:19) 18/32. Occurs as 'the Thing itself' in early Quaker writings.
thirst after righteousness 13/2–7; after the creatures 12/26–27; after Lord the Creator and his Son Jesus 12/26–29
time (1): contrasted with timeless or eternal: 21/7 175/39 574/26–575/3
time (2): one's lifetime 143/39–144/7 see also **prize your time**
time (3): The period for preaching the sermon was protected by law in the 17th C. and was measured by an hour-glass on the pulpit. Examples are extant: 148/27–149/32. Fox's three interruptions, see Nickalls 771 (ignore p.76, but see instead p. 148/29)
traditions: religious traditions; see also **Roman Catholicism:**
people to be brought off traditions to Christ 50/12–14 Roman Catholic traditions: how established 343/11–344/37
transgression:
Adam's 'entrance into transgression' 31/20–22
the Spirit of God is 'transgressed in man' 28/26–28
'hearts through transgression were become as a wilderness' 32/13
'translation' (= transference) (*Col.* 1:13 KJV) see also **conversion; redeem:**

in Christ's Power and Light, translation (into the Kingdom) from
the power of Satan is known 283/13–18 367/21–27

travail (for); sometimes 'travel' (17th C.): to labour, as in child-birth:
'travail for the Seed and yet bring forth nothing but strife' 417/24–27

tree: GF 'stiff as a tree and pure as a bell' 502/34–35

troubles; see also **temptations:**

(the Father) 'deliverer out of the six and seven troubles' (*Job* 5:19)
277/10–14

Truth: see also **Principle (2); Spirit of Truth;** pp.xx/22–xxi/9 cf.
53/27–31 282/18–24:

(A) Christ is the Truth 35/7–19

Grace and Truth come by Jesus (*Jn* 1:17) 12/38–13/1 272/24

'is the unchangeable Truth ... the Light of Christ Jesus'
13/14–19

God is a God of Truth 212/32

is everlasting 19/1 326/27 574/31–575/3

is 'the girdle' (*Eph.* 6:14) 176/17

is in the heart 34/10–12

is over all 369/2

is 'come into' 341/22–25

is possessed 204/21–22

is settled in 370/2

can be 'run out from' 176/24–25

is to be worshipped in (*Jn* 4:23) 35/15–19

is without (i.e. beyond) time—belongs to a different world 574/
26–575/3 has a savour 548/18–19

the Devil abides not in the Truth 444/2–14

is confirmed by the Scriptures 302/10

is renowned (*Ezek.* 16:14) 167/12–15 (cf. 640/27–30)

(B) the Truth of the Lord answers the Witness of God 313/6

came over (= overcame) all 48/12–13 76/1–3

comes to reign 176/17

guides people to Christ from sin 48/20–21

'operates' in people's hearts 435/8

reaches in all hearts 80/13 with God's Truth 438/3

'sounds abroad in the hearts of men' 640/27–30

spreads over the nation 285/12

(C) believe in it 312/35
'Be valiant for the Truth' 263/11
'Live all in the peaceable Truth' 595/29–33
love it 95/14–16 232/20–22
practise it 170/12–13
receive it 80/22–25 232/20–22
spread it abroad 263/6

types, figures and shadows: Outward features and events which belonged to the first Covenant—such as the priests, the sabbath, the Temple, and Jerusalem—were deemed by NT writers to be anticipations of their later spiritual counterparts in the new Covenant. Thus Adam is the 'type' of Jesus ('the second Adam'—Fox, *Rom.* 5:14). The later, fuller manifestations are the 'antitypes'. Jerusalem, for example, was said to foreshadow, or be a 'shadow' or 'figure' of 'the heavenly Jerusalem' (*Heb.* 12:23, the spiritual city). Fox's special use of 'figures' (see **figure (1)**) relates to his inward/outward, within/without categories, not to the time sequence of type-antitype. Christ is 'the Substance' of the shadows and is seen as fulfilling the types, figures and shadows of the OT and as ending them.

'Typology,' writes Gwyn, 'is the chief way in which the NT writers understand the life, death and resurrection of Jesus Christ as fulfilling the writings of Moses and the prophets. . . (and) the relationship of the first Covenant mediated by Moses (to) the new Convenant mediated by Jesus'. Fox does not see these correspondencies as allegories or simply as literary devices. He makes a historical connection. He understands Jesus Christ as the Word of God 'incarnating' in his life, death and resurrection, and as 'fulfilling' the history of Israel. And, further, 'in his revelation within the individual (man and woman) the same Word *recapitulates* history': he '*re-enacts* his fulfilment of the first Covenant through the (obedient) individual's personal experience'. There is obviously here, Gwyn comments, 'an overarching concern for the community of the Church and a strong engagement with history' (pp.96–97, my italics); see also **history of mankind:**

see especially 31/12–32/40 367/7–27 and Gwyn, chapter 5. Also 14/8–18/8 27/17–28/6

Fox writes a 'book' about types, etc. 416/1–8

clean beasts offered up (as types of Jesus Christ) 31/35–42
all ended by Christ the Substance 32/24–29 367/7–26
unity: see also **'Theology'; Being:**
is come 204/26–27
in the Life 175/19–21 437/8
in the Light 173/19–20
in the Spirit (with God, Christ and one another) 103/29–34 228/
15–19
'unity with the creation' 2/13–14 110/10–11
ministry and unity 17/28–29
universality of the Light of Christ within (*Jn* 1:9) see **Grace of God;
Light (A); measure (A); the Witness of God**
vanity and young people (*Eccl.* 11:10):
'young people go together into vanity' 3/20
veil: sometimes 'vail' (17th cent.) : anything that separates man from
God (cf. *Exod.* 34:29–35 2 *Cor.* 3:13–16 *Heb.* 9:3); 'I discerned . . .
what it was that did veil me' 14/21, 35 23/4 'that which would cloud
and veil from the presence of Christ' 15/4–5
victory (spiritual victory over sin):
(faith gives) 'victory over sin', and **access to God** (qv) 318/12–15
violence: see **social testimonies**
virgin (1): virgin birth; see **birth (3)**
virgin (2): the virgin mind, soul and spirit (*Mt.* 25:1–12, the wise
virgins): the power of God is the keeper who keeps the virgin minds,
souls and spirits from defilement Ep. 265 p.293 8.5/3–17 7/1–5 Ep.
372 p.469 8.208/41–209/2
The Light turns your minds 'towards God, where the pure Babe is
born in the virgin mind' Ep. 56, p.55 7.71/23–24
visitation: 338/25–33 see also **Day (1)**
Voice; the inward Voice: see also **Christ: God; wilderness (2):**
of Christ 666/1–3,8–11
of God and Christ 87/38–40 123/17–29
of God 11/18–20 'Then O! then I heard a Voice . . .'
is to be obeyed 200/1–4
in hearing the Son we hear the Father also 666/1–4
'the (spiritual) graves opened and the dead heard the voice of God'
122/35

the thundering Voice 477/26–33

'a true voice' 25/22 cf. 25/17–18 a false voice

'All must first know the voice crying in the wilderness of their hearts'
(*Lk.* 3:4ff.) 32/11–13, the call to repentance 32/11–13

wait(ing) upon God or the Lord (*Ps.* 62:1 etc, *Isa.* 40:31); see also
silent meeting; worship:

(A) waiting 'when they do not speak words' 359/34–35

(C) 'wait upon the Lord whatever condition you be in' 12/37–38
176/6–17

'if you do, there is a promise to you' 13/1–2

wait: 'in that which convinced you' (i.e. the Light) 228/14

'in the fear of God for the Seed (Christ)' 337/36–338/3

'in the Grace and Truth' 12/38–13/1

'in the measure of Life' 175/19–20

'Waiting in the Light you will receive the power of God' 176/13

'upon the Lord in his Power and Spirit' 449/14–15

'for Wisdom from God' 173/6

'walk cheerfully': 'Be patterns, be examples, . . . *then* [NB the con-
dition] you will walk cheerfully over the world. . .' ('over', see
Vocabulary) 263/27–31 see also **Light (1) (C)**

wanderers: those 'who wander from the will and Power of God, in
their own wills and earthly minds' 265/28 cf. **stars (3):** wandering
stars

war (1): see **social testimonies** (A) (12)

War (2): 'the Lamb's War': 'against spiritual wickedness' (*Eph.* 6:12):
the war between the Lamb, Christ, and his saints (the true Christians) on the one side, and 'the Beast', the **Devil** (qv) on the other
(Ep.138 p.108/13–16 7.133/19–23). Based upon Fox's understanding of *Rev.* 14–19

Nickalls omits specific mention of the Lamb's war, but it embraces
all opposition to 'the false church' that was set up in the world after
the apostles' time, and to all oppressors and evil-doers generally.
The weapons are spiritual (2 *Cor.* 10:4)—'the Sword of the Spirit,
the Word of his mouth' (*Eph.* 6:17 *Rev.* 19:15): see also **church (1);
night of the apostasy; social testimonies** (A) (12) and (B) (5): 197/
23–198/25 (OC)

'Stand in that . . . Power, Life, Light . . . by which you take away the

occasion of wars; and so know a Kingdom that has no end. Fight for
that, with spiritual weapons, which takes away the occasion of the
carnal [weapons]. And there gather men to war, as many as you can,
and set up as many as you can with these weapons.' EJ 202/46–203/5
1.390/13–19

water and bread of Life (*Jn* 4:10ff. 6:32 ff.) 18/14–16 see **Bread of Life**

Way/ways: see also **Christ (1)** (A); **Light (1)** (A):
(1) the Way (*Jn* 14:6)
see especially 189/16–23
is everlasting 13/17–19
is within 114/1

ways (2): 'rough and crooked ways' (*Lk.* 3:5)
are inward 32/4–10 45/32–46/2
are in man's heart 16/15–17
must be made smooth and plain 16/14–17 32/4–10 113/31–114/1

ways (3): the world's ways 104/15 107/10

wilderness (1): see also **world (1)** and **(2); woman** (the Church):
'the world is like a briery thorny wilderness' 33/33–35

wilderness (2): 'a barren wilderness' (*Isa.* 32:15); see also **God (B)**.
is in the heart 10/24–29 13/7–10 283/39
'all must first know the voice crying in the wilderness' (John the
Baptist's call to repentance *Jn* 1:23) 32/11–12

will (1): will of God; see also **providence of God: prosper:**
see especially 193–5 (letter to OC)
(all things) stand in his will 66/6–33
the power of God crucifies all that is contrary to it 18/5–8

will (2): the earthly will; see also **earth**
(A) its wisdom is 'devilish' 17/32 see **wisdom (1)**
      must perish 17/29–32
(B) seeks its liberty 17/38–18/1
      reigns in its own knowledge 17/29–32
      wars against the Spirit of God 17/33–18/5

will (3): man's will 23/7, self-will 10/32: 'Now do not think that I hold
free will here, man's free will. I speak of that which is contrary to
man's will . . . the Light will keep your wills in *subjection*.' 4.20/
39–42

wine: the bread and wine: see **sacraments**

winter (*Mt.* 24:20, *Mk* 13:18): (fig.) a time of spiritual trial; see **fly** (=flee): 'after[wards] you may feel winter storms' 283/36–42

wisdom (1): men's reasonings and calculations for their own ends: man's wisdom 194/30–33 (OC)

'earthly, sensual, devilish wisdom' (*Jas.* 3:15) 311/9–10

Wisdom (2): heavenly wisdom; see also **Wisdom of God:**
is 'from above' (*Jas.* 3:17) 311/10–13

Wisdom (3) of God: the ordering Principle=Christ (1 *Cor.* 1:24); see also **Christ (2) (A); Gospel order; order; professions; Wisdom (2); Word (10) of Wisdom:**
see especially 173/5–40

(A) is Christ (1 *Cor.* 1:24) 38/34–38 see **Word (2)**

is that 'by which all things were made and created' (=the Word) 311/12–13 322/4–5 439/21–22

is 'gentle' and 'easy to be entreated' (*Jas.* 3:17) 311/11–12

is a gift to those who 'live in the Lord's power and life' 193/25–26

is received in the Light 175/9–10

by which (=whom) right knowledge of virtues of the creatures is known 29/8–10 see **professions**

from whom right knowledge of all things is received 38/37–38

(B) calms men's spirits 193/18–19

frustrates men's ends 193/18

nourishes 173/5–9

orders 173/9–29 322/3–7 see **order**

rules 173/17

(C) 'Live in the Lord's power and Life, then to thee he will give Wisdom' 193/17–40 194/28–29

'Now he that believes in the Light . . . [receives] the Wisdom' 175/8–9 (corrected)

'with it you may order all things under your hands' 322/6–7 439/23–24

wait (to) 'receive his wisdom from Above' 173/6 322/3–4 175/19–27

'the treasures of Wisdom are opened' 204/31–33

(justices are to) 'mind God's wisdom' 439/19–24

Witness (1) of God, the: the Spirit of God and Truth in every one (1 *Jn*

5:6–10) 221/38

is quenched (1 *Thess.* 5:19) by hypocrisy etc. 354/35–36

'was raised up in him' 157/27–28

is reached by the Life and Light 281/13–19

(words) 'reached to the Witness of God in every one' 281/13–21 302/ 3–11 (see *Jer.* 31:34)

witness (2): the practical expression of a testimony: see **social testimonies**

Woman: the Woman: = the Church: see also **Church (2):**

The Israel of the Old Covenant is the Woman (*Jer.* 31:21, 22) and the Husband is God (see also *Isa.* 54:4–6). The NT parallels are 'the Lamb's Bride and Wife' (*Rev.* 21:9). See also 'Christ's Spouse' (1611 interpretation of *Song of Solomon*), and 'the woman in the wilderness' (*Rev.* 12:1, 5, 6, 13, 15–17, the true Church. On this Hebrew usage, Fox based two unusual interpretations:-

'Let the Woman [i.e. the Church] learn in silence' (1 *Tim.* 2:11) *Doctr.* 77–82 4.104/7–8

'"The earth" was helping the Woman' (*Rev.* 12:16): i.e. the world's laws were being applied justly on Fox's behalf, thus helping the Church 682/7–30

women: the place of women in the church (*Joel* 2:28–29, *Gal.* 3:28); see also **gospel order; women's meetings** see Nickalls's index 775; **ministry (9); social testimonies; soul:**

see especially 666/27–668/20 *Epistles* 35, 248, 308, 320, 351, 419; 24/9–20 464/1–8 *Doctr.* pp. 77–82 4.104–110

Word (1): the Word of faith (*Rom.* 10:8, *Deut.* 31:12):

sanctifies, makes holy and reconciles to God Ep. 372, p. 469/14–16 8.209/9–11

Word (2): the Word of God (*Jn* 1:1–4) see also **Bible (1):**

see especially 295/28–296/31

(A) Christ is the Word (*Jn* 1:14, 1 *Jn* 5:7, *Rev.* 19:13) 13/25 274/ 33–34 472/2

is the 'incorruptible Seed' (= Christ) (1 *Pet.* 1:23) 24/11

'The Word is God' (*Jn* 1:1) 322/17

'In him was Life, to wit, the Word . . .' (*Jn* 1:4) 295/32–33 296/14 303/10

'is like a hammer and a fire' (*Jer.* 23:29) 122/23–26

is divine, not natural 471/26–30

'lives and abides for ever' (1 *Pet.* 1:23) 24/12 531/10–11

is a message to be declared 123/23–26

the Bible is not the Word of God 145/28–32 146/8–10 159/26–28

see also **Bible (1)**

(B) 'became flesh (*Jn* 1:14) but not corrupt flesh' (see *Acts* 2:27, 13:35 *Ps.* 16:10) 336/7

'born again . . . by the Word of God' (1 *Pet.* 1:23) 531/9–10

'burns up' the 'briery brambly nature' 331/27–28

divides (i.e. distinguishes) good thoughts and words from the bad (*Heb.* 4:12) 332/16–22

fulfills the Scriptures 159/26–28

'effectually operates in the hearts of men' (1 *Thess.* 2:13) 400/16–17

reconciles to the Scripture, to God, and one another 332/17–22

sanctifies 2/12

(C) 'in the living, unmoveable Word of God, dwell' 340/10–11

(we) 'must know it in (the) heart and mouth' (*Deut.* 30:14) 332/20

feed of (on) 'the milk of the Word' (1 *Pet.* 2:2) 368/36–38

Word (3) of Life (*Jn* 6:68, 1 *Jn* 1:1 *Phil.* 2:16):

abides and lives 368/33–38

is eternal 276/17–18

is powerful 179/25

is declared 33/33–37 39/14 91/37–92/1 . . . 276/17–18 292/29 304/18

is **divided** (qv) 271/2

Word (4) of the Lord (and of Christ) = prophetic words given as a message uttered as from the Lord: 96/22–23 123/3–33 124/23–24 125/22–23 (divided= preached) see also **words (2)**

Word (5) of patience (*Rev.* 3:8–10):

'keep the Word of patience which was before the world began' 405/12

Word (6) of power (*Heb.* 1:3 4:12) 27/37

Word (7) of prophecy (2 *Pet.* 1:19) 40/1–5 see **prophecy**

Word (8) of reconciliation (2 *Cor.* 5:19);

and Life 22/3–4

declared 39/14 271/11–14

Word (9) of Truth (*Eph.* 1:13, *Jas.* 1:18) GF's commonest summaries
of his message are 'the Truth' 95/8 'the everlasting Truth' 91/30 'the
Truth of God' 80/2 (see also **Truth**) and 'the Word of Life' 91/6–7
92/1 102/7,8 (not 'world') 110/15 150/6 158/6–7

Word (10) of Wisdom (1 *Cor.* 12:8); see also **Wisdom (3) of God:**
is received as we come into subjection to the will of God 28/2–5
and of Power made the creation 27/37–38 28/15–19 29/7–12
opens all things 28/5
reveals the works of the creation 27/35–28/6

words (1): mere words, not based on experience:
'airy notions' 19/34–38 'great swelling words of vanity' 6.239/21
(people) 'fed upon words' 19/33–34

words (2) of (= from) **God;** see also **Bible (1)** and **(2): prophecy (2):**
the Scriptures are the words (not *the* Word) of God 145/28–32 146/
8–10
were heard by the prophets . . . in the silence before they spoke forth
the Scriptures 359/33–360/11

words (3) and life: see **social testimonies** (A) integrity (A) (2)

world (1): the world = the sea (*Jude* 13): see also **sea; wilderness:**
'are known by their tempestuous spirits' Ep. 499/20 8.243/39 33/36–
34/2
'the world' made a noise like the great 'raging waves' 14/24–26

world (2): the people of 'the world'; see also **religion (2); righteousness
(5); worship (2):**
see especially 472/5–18 their 'righteousness'
people as they are without God 2/15–20
the world's hearts are in the creatures 309/34
are at ease in worldly comforts 12/32–35 200/10–22
their knowledge is in the flesh 309/35, is fleshly 10/34–35
their minds are not renewed 309/35
Christ spoke against the works of the world 68/22–23

worship (1): the true worship; (*Jn* 4: 23–24); see also **meeting (1);
singing; wait:**
is free in the Spirit to all men 417/5–8
is in the Truth 35/7–19 417/5–23 (*Jn* 4:24)

worship (2): the world's 35/15 36/1–14; see **world (2).**

Social Testimonies and Witness

(= Christian living, personal and corporate)

Under this heading are gathered many of the testimonies and forms of witness through which the early Quaker Christian faith was expressed. I have assumed a broad distinction between testimonies as verbal or written statements of positions adopted in relation to specific aspects of Christian living, whereas a witness is an action taken as overt expression of such views. The distinctive all-round Christian character of Quaker living sprang from the practice of bringing the whole of life to the Light in obedience to the teaching of Jesus (see **Light (2)**).

(A) The Character of a True Christian

Summary
Act faithfully in two ways —
(a) *'inwardly to God ...'*
    (1) Be honest, (2) having integrity, (3) be loving, (4) pure, (5) serious, (6) preferring simplicity, (7) be sincere, (8) truthful,
(b) *'... and outwardly to man'* 1/27–2/2
    (9) honouring God in all men and women, (10) just in one's dealings with others, (11) just in administering the law, (12) a peace-maker, (13) upright (=righteous) in dealings with others, (14) acting responsibly towards the creation (humankind, animals, plants, inanimate matter)

Detailed Applications

(a) *Inward faithfulness*
(1) Be honest and innocent: 2/5–6 216/10–11; honest-hearted 445/17; making restitution 41/16–27
    Against deceit 2/5; 'changeable words' 2/5; crime and lawlessness 460/10–21; theft and robbery 324/20–21; burglary 216/1–11

(2) Show integrity (faithfulness in all things): Fox commends *Job* 27:1–9 166/23–33 311/30–35 see *Prov.* 20:7 *Ps.* 25:21. Of the heart 258/20. In words and life 173/30–31 410/12–13 'I was the same in life as I was in words' 528/4–12

(3) Be loving: (Do unto others etc. (*Mt.* 7:12 *Lk.* 6:31)); see **love** (3)–(5) 'We love all people and are the enemies of none' 439/1–6 Against looting of wrecks and neglecting to rescue people (Cornwall) 364/1–26; poverty 373/25–30; treatment of slaves 598/20–599/6

(4) Be pure (*Mt.* 5:8): as a bell 502/33–34 see **pure**

(5) Be serious: seriousness of mind (sobriety); 'the meek and quiet spirit' 205/17; children to be taught sobriety 38/9 Against wantonness—root meaning, undisciplined. Various obsolete meanings: 1/18–24 perhaps, here, lewdly; 2/8 self-indulgent, through using the **creatures** (qv) wastefully; 2/16–17 satisfying the lust (i.e. gluttonous); public feasts 37/31–36; games (wrestling, football) 337/33–34; May-day games that trained people up to vanity and looseness 37/32–35; mountebanks (sellers of quack medicines) 38/6–7; music 'against all sorts of music' 38/5; plays 37/32–36; wakes (=public feasts) 37/31–36

(6) Seek simplicity (2 *Cor* 1:12): 353/33 the simplicity that is in Christ (2 *Cor.* 11:3) Against fashions of the world (vain adornment of the body) 205/18–206/35; vanity 38/6–11; destroying the simplicity 353/33

(7) Be sincere; godly sincerity (2 *Cor.* 1:12) 400/30–36 Against conventional greetings 36/19–20 250/4–10; bowing and 'scraping' (to draw the foot back in making obeisance *Chamb.*) 36/20–22; hypocrisy in politics 349/36 353/29–354/16; making a pretence 75/27–33

(8) Be truthful: 'Yea and nay' (*Mt.* 5:37 *Jas.* 5:12) Honesty and truthfulness 169/20–170/5; keeps his word 2/1–7 386/27–387/16 389/1–6; in commerce and trade 37/36–38/3 Against bargaining 169/20–31; Royal pardons 701/3–10 701/25–702/5; swearing oaths 181/28–182/13 (*Jas* 5:12) 244/32–245/14 in courts of law 466/9–467/29 498/12–499/15

(b) Outward faithfulness

(9) Loving and peaceful personal and social relationships:
Honour God in every man and woman:
For equal status of every man and woman, see **women** and **marriage** and (B)(2) below:
Against disharmony within marriage and between neighbours 520/35–522/6
Against adultery, fornication, and abusing oneself with mankind (1 *Cor.* 5:9–11 6:9): 'Keep your bodies clean from all fornication, adultery, and uncleanness . . .; for no adulterer nor fonicator has any part in the Kingdom of God' (1 *Cor.* 6:9 see **Kingdom of God**). 'Such go from that of God in themselves, and quench the Spirit of God in themselves' Ep. 168 7.156/24–30.
Social classes and barriers 'There is no respect of persons with God' *(Rom.* 2:11 *Deut.* 10:17).
Against social classes and social barriers. 'Thee' and 'thou': 'I was required to thee and thou all men and women, without respect for rich or poor, great or small' 36/15–18, 27–32 242/24–33 354/2–9 416/9–35 *(The Battledore)* 498/3–499/18. The use of titles (so called) 464/11; social pride 36/35–36 205/35–37. The 'world's honour' 36/15–37/25 200/10–22 (OC) 242/19–33 246/1–10. 'Hat-honour' 36, 37 242/24–33 243/5–32. The existence of want is inconsistent with true religion 35/20–26 373/14–21, 29–30.
The care of poor Friends' families (apprenticeships) 555/30–556/39

(10) Do justly
Employers and servants in 17th C. 'extended family' 26/27–29 38/11–16; employees to give honest service 26/29–30
Against oppression: fixing wages too low 26/25–30; fraudulent dealing 41/16–27; excessive excise charges 49/5–9

(11) Administer the law justly
For good government and magistracy 460/10–21 Judges and justices: true and merciful justice 37/26–28 66/9–22;
Against injustice 577/27–30 secures justice 66/23–35; corruption of judges (gifts and rewards) 66/16; Royal pardons 701/3–10, 25–702/5 excessive punishment 65/28–32 66/9–22; long periods in prison 66/35–67/4; swearing of oaths 244/24–245/14 422/23–423/3

(12) Be peace-makers 'Seek peace and ensue it' (1 *Pet.* 3:11 *Jas.*
4:1–2) 399/1–2, 5; 1660 Peace Testimony 398–404; GF lived in
'the virtue of that Life and Power which takes away the occasion
of all wars' 65/9–10 67/11–21 197/23–198/25 see also **war(1)**
Against resistance to evil *(Mt.*5:38–48); see also **cross (7)–(11)**;
against doing violence to any man 157/35 381/1–9; violence for
political ends 356/21–357/36 358/1–40; 'wars and fightings' 398/
24–404/10 (the Peace Testimony); 'they that pretend (=claim) to
fight for Christ' 357/12–24; 'strife and separation' (among
Friends) EJ 449/8; 'wars, strife' 65/14–15; putting people to death
for religion 419/4–5 see also testimonies about true religion,
below, and **cross (6)–(11)**

(13) Be upright (=righteous) 400/42; zealous for righteousness 386/
5–15 Against cozening (=deceiving) in trade and commerce
37/36–38 202/10 (201/19–202/15); against deceit and well-mean-
ing deception 570/21–33; seeks no redress from persecutors 254/
18–29 415/22–25; trusts in the Lord 505/9–14; patient under trial
381/20–23 see **cross (6)–(12); patience**

(14) Act responsibly towards the creation; see also **creation**
Eating and drinking: 'meat' = food in 17th C. usage, see *Gen.*
1:29(KJV). For health only 2/7–10; he uses the creatures 'in their
places' *(Gen.*1:28, 29) 2/7–14; see also 'dominion over all' 667/
38–39; for temperance in using alcoholic drinks 37/30. The true
fast: implied in 727/5–10 see **fast (1)**
Against excessive eating and drinking ('devouring the creation')
2/7–20; the forbidding of 'meats' (foods) 343/15; drunkenness
27/1; sale of harmful amounts of alcoholic drinks 37/26–30 Ep.
381; the misuse of the creation 439/21–24; the wasting and
destruction of the creation Ep.200; the extermination of species
'Leave all the creatures behind you as you found them, which
God has given to serve all nations and generations' *Doctr.* 274/
28–30 5.321/8–9; the mis-treatment of animals 376/18–29. The
false fast, see **fast (2)**. Against the drinking of healths (the first
Quaker witness) 3/1–15, Ep.1698 p.3 (refusal to drink the king's
health 1660).

(B) The Characteristics of 'True Religion' (Jas.1:27) 35/20–23 and of 'the True Church' Fellowship 283/19–28.

see also **baptism (2); church (2); Gospel order; meeting (1); ministers; priests; religion (1); righteousness; sacraments; war (1)** and **(2); women.**

(1) Harmony among Friends 281/3–21

(2) Marriage: biblical precedents for Quaker practice 500/25–501/6; harmony in marriage 320/30–35; procedure among Friends 519/7–37; 576/32–577/24 'God, who is a Spirit, joins with his Spirit, Power and Light. This joining is in the Covenant of God. All such marriages are honourable in all things, for their bed is not defiled' Ep.264 7.335/18–20 partners in serving God 506/5–17 621/36–622/8; **meet helps** (qv) i.e. men and women as helps meet (= fit, suitable) for one another

(3) Meetings for worship: see also **meetings (1); worship (1)**
freedom of worship 558/21–560/18
the NT practice of worship (1 *Cor.* 14:30,31) 69/2–11 563/18–565/6
silent waiting upon God, 'the heavenly supper' (*Rev.* 3:20) 261/24–31 359/33–35 'Keep your testimony for your . . . worship in Spirit and in truth, that Christ has set up' 8.34/1–3
Against all forms of worship not 'in the Power' 35/20–38

(4) Meetings for other purposes; for travelling ministers 340, 341; for condemnations 533/1–6; see Nickalls's index for Monthly, Quarterly, Yearly Meetings etc. 775. The spiritual purpose of monthly meetings 520/35–521/6 525/8–15 528/1–23. Other forms of meetings were held, e.g. meetings for testimonies, 'threshing meetings' and arranged disputes with opponents, and meetings to hear epistles from abroad; see also **meetings (2)**

(5) Testimonies against the World's/False Religions
augmentations 207/24
church festivals: Christmas 359/6
ceremonies, Jewish 36/1
days, holy, observance of 36/8–9 669/27–32
divination, payment for 39/12–13
Easter reckonings 207/24
fables, heathenish 36/2

Appendices

1. Chronological Bibliography of Works on George Fox's Teaching additional to those referred to in the Preface

The work of a few British Friends between about 1830 and 1850 is still useful and deserves to be known. They re-published journals of some of the leading early Friends, for instance: *William Dewsbury,* Edward Smith (1846); *William Caton* and *John Burnyeat,* A.R.Barclay (1839); *Letters to Early Friends.* A. R. Barclay (1841); and *John Whitehead,* Thomas Chalk (1852). These comparatively straight forward accounts of their conversions and their letters to one another reveal clearly the tenor of Fox's message and how it affected them, and, equally importantly, how in due time they became messengers in their turn. That the message has the power of calling forth its own bearers is one of its vital characteristics. Thus in writings of the first wave of travelling ministers one finds confirmation of insights into the nature of the Quaker Christian teaching which are won with some difficulty from Fox's voluminous prose. Comparisons show that Quaker preachers and teachers later in the 17th century were expounding a significantly different message.

John Wilhelm Rowntree: *Essays and Addresses* (London: Headley 1905). Introductory sketch and the lecture on 'The Rise of Quakerism in Yorkshire', pp.2–32.

Thomas C. Kennedy's *History and Quaker Renaissance: The Vision of John Wilhelm Rowntree, Journal of the Friends Historical Society,* vol. 55, pp. 35–56 (1983–84), contains a valuable assessment of his pioneer work.

A. Neave Brayshaw: *The Quakers: their Story and Message* (London: Allen & Unwin, 1938 Sessions, York, 3rd edn. 1953 rpt. 1982) Brayshaw was the first to use Fox's *Epistles.* Although his contribution to the recovery of the message was not substantial, his books contain much relevant material, especially on Fox himself: *The Personality of George Fox* (Allenson: London 1933, revised).

L. Violet Hodgkin: *A Day-Book of Counsel and Comfort* (London: Macmillan 1937) A selection of passages from the *Epistles* (1698)

144

arranged for daily reading.

Rachel H. King: *George Fox and the Light Within 1650–60* (Philadelphia: Friends Book Store 1940). This first academic study of one aspect of Fox's teaching contains useful insights.

The above mentioned books are out of print but are occasionally available second-hand.

*   *   *

Lewis Benson: *Prophetic Quakerism* (printed by the author 1943, reprinted by the Friends Home Service Committee, London, 1951: reprinted in *The Quaker Vision,* below); *Catholic Quakerism* (printed by the author 1966; reprinted by Philadelphia Y.M. (1968)).

These two studies represent Benson's critical examination of the nature of the early Quaker movement as understood by Rufus M. Jones (1863–1947), whose views prevailed during the first half of the twentieth century. Benson re-discovered Fox's teaching about the universal (catholic) and prophetic character of early Christianity and early Quakerism.

Also by Lewis Benson, and all published by the New Foundation Fellowship:

What did George Fox teach about Christ? (New Foundation, Gloucester, 1975) A transcription of three addresses.

The Quaker Vision (1979): Six articles on the relevance of Fox's message for today; the conception of the Church; two on universal aspects of Fox's thought; 'The Power of God and the Power of Man'; and 'On Being Moved by the Spirit to Minister in Public Worship';

The Truth is Christ (1981): Four articles on: 'Prophetic Quakerism' (1943); 'The Religionless Christianity of George Fox'; 'the Church as the New Covenant people'; and 'Friends and Truth';

Notes on George Fox (1981): Benson's research tool—passages from Fox's published and unpublished writings, classified under hundreds of headings: with an index by Arthur Windsor. Indispensable for students.

*   *   *

Joseph Pickvance: *George Fox's Use of the Word 'Seed'* (1949), *Journal Friends Historical Society,* Vol. 41, pp. 25–28. Surveys the evidence for thinking that Fox did not use 'Seed' in relation to the parable of the sower or to growth of any kind.

Joseph Pickvance: *George Fox on the Light of Christ Within* (1978). An exposition of the first part of the early Quaker message, supported by many quotations from Fox. With a brief biography.

Called to Be a People (1985): Five studies written by a team for use with small groups: 'The Word of God'; 'Obedience and the People of God'; 'God is Light'; 'The Church'; 'Peace with God'. With Bible references to passages used by Fox and quotations from him to show how he used them.

Michael Langford: *Making a Fresh Start with Fox and the Bible* (1987). A useful introduction to the biblical character of Fox's message and the language in which it is expressed.

All published by the New Foundation Fellowship, 4 Brunswick Square, Gloucester, England, GL1 1UG; also available through Quaker bookshops.

*   *   *

Douglas Gwyn: *Apocalypse of the Word* (Richmond, Indiana; Friends United Press, 1987). The most substantial work on the Quaker Christian message to date. It covers many aspects with new insights. To help with the less familiar topics a 12-session parallel Study Guide with the same title, by Douglas Gwyn and edited by Patricia Edwards-De Lancey, is also available.

T. Canby Jones: *The Power of the Lord is over all,* (Richmond, Indiana; Friends United Press, 1989). Contains a selection from each of Fox's four hundred epistles (1698 edition); with a valuable introduction and comprehensive indexes.

Quaker Religious Thought. The Quaker Theological Discussion Group, which was established in America in 1958, publishes this twice-yearly periodical. The normal format is a main address with critical comments by two or three other members. In addition to being a valuable Quaker ecumenical forum, the QTDG reveals through *QRT,* with its wide-ranging subjects, how research into the early Quaker faith has developed and deepened. Of the following selection, Vol.16 contains what has proved to be the most significant single contribution by Lewis Benson.

Vol. 1 No, 1 1960 The Early Quaker Vision of the Church—Lewis Benson

Vol.4 No. 1 1962 The Bible in George Fox and Contemporary Quakerism—T. Canby Jones

Vol.12 No. 2 1970 That of God in Every Man—Lewis Benson

Vol.16 Nos 1 & 2 1974–75 Christ as Prophet—Lewis Benson

Vol.22 No. 3 1987 Fox's Message—Lisa Kuenning

2. Editions of George Fox's *Journal*

In the strict sense, Fox's *Journal* is the version dictated by him to his stepson-in-law Thomas Lower at Worcester and Swarthmoor Hall between 1674 and 1676. All but the lost first sixteen pages of the original manuscripts are in Friends House Library, London. These, the Spence MSS, were printed *verbatim et literatim* in 1911 as *The Journal of George Fox* in two volumes by the Cambridge University Press. It is referred to as 'the Cambridge Edition'. This unpunctuated version was not deliberately edited beyond the inevitable realisation of Fox's speech in Lower's own wayward spelling and his phonetic south country renderings of Fox's north country pronunciations. Very little of the MS is in Fox's own handwriting. Norman Penney added invaluable notes.

From the Cambridge edition are descended:- Norman Penney's edition (London: Dent 1924, which is illustrated with Robert Spence's etchings, and Dent's Everyman edition, which is unillustrated); and John L. Nickalls's 1952 edition (CUP), and the 1975 edition, for which the footnotes were substantially revised. Both editions share the same title and end at 1675.

The principal edition is Thomas Ellwood's (1694). He filled out Thomas Lower's text with epistles and papers at appropriate points, and composed the narrative after 1675 from Fox's autobiographical material and itinerary journals. From Ellwood are descended:- the first two of the eight volumes of the American 1831 edition of Fox's *Works;* and the English edition of 1852 by Wilson Armstead which was revised by Daniel Pickard in 1891 as 'the Bicentenary Edition'. The last named is occasionally available second-hand. It includes all the documents inserted by Ellwood. All single volume editions smaller than folio have been more or less drastically abridged. Modernisation of spelling and punctuation is always necessary, but what further editing is justifiable is a matter for discussion as standards in scholarship change. Ellwood smoothed curious country expressions and omitted puzzling incidents. Thus in Nickalls Fox 'sounds the Day of the Lord' on Pendle Hill: in Ellwood's genus of editions, he does not (see **sound(5)**).

He also altered or omitted words, some of which are of theological significance. For this reason students need to check important points with the Cambridge edition. Nickalls reversed many but not all of Ellwood's changes. Yet without the latter's labours Fox's journal would not be recognised as a religious classic.

3. Samuel Tuke's *Selections from the Epistles of George Fox (1858)*

Fox's Epistle Nos. corresponding to Tuke's Page Nos.

Ep. No.	p. no.	Ep. No.	p. no.	Ep. No.	p. no.	Ep. No.	p. no.
16	22	128	34	283	60	376	86
17	23	138	35	293	61	377	87
24	24	148	36	304	63	380	89
27	25	153	38	336	64	384	92
38	26	175	40	340	65	386	94
51	27	186	41	355	67	391	96
64	28	189	42	360	70	396	100
80	29	200	43	361	72	398	102
102	30	216	50	364	74	399	105
105	31	245	52	366	76	405	108
114	32	249	54	368	79	407	110
120	33	250	57	369	81	412	111
127	33	256	58	370	83	420	113
		268	59				

4. Recovering George Fox's Quaker Christian Message

In the section on this topic (p.29), it was suggested that the message could be pieced together by linking the topics of which it is composed by means of the Concordance. Although possible, this is a lengthy business. Cassette tape-recordings of a reconstruction of most of the topics are available for purchase or loan from the New Foundation Fellowship through Quaker Home Service, Friends House, Euston Road, London, England NW1 2BJ, or from the Fellowship in other countries.